Voodoo Priests, Noble Savages, and Ozark Gypsies

Missouri Biography Series   William E. Foley, Editor

VOODOO PRIESTS, NOBLE SAVAGES, AND OZARK GYPSIES

The Life of Folklorist
Mary Alicia Owen

GREG OLSON

UNIVERSITY OF MISSOURI PRESS   COLUMBIA AND LONDON

Copyright © 2012 by
The Curators of the University of Missouri
University of Missouri Press, Columbia, Missouri 65201
Printed and bound in the United States of America
All rights reserved
5 4 3 2 1   16 15 14 13 12

Cataloging-in-Publication data available from the Library of Congress.
ISBN 978-0-8262-1996-1

♾™ This paper meets the requirements of the
American National Standard for Permanence of Paper
for Printed Library Materials, Z39.48, 1984.

Jacket design: Whitney Fenzel
Composition: Jennifer Cropp
Printing and binding: Thomson-Shore, Inc.
Typefaces: Palatino and LinotypeZapfino

For Rebecca Schroeder,
who introduced me to the world
and work of Mary Alicia Owen

Contents

Acknowledgments

This book has gone through a variety of incarnations before finally reaching its present form, and many people offered help and advice along the way. I would like to acknowledge my gratitude to Robert Collins and to my fellow seminar students at the University of Missouri–Columbia for their ideas and suggestions on the earliest version of this work. Later, I was very fortunate to receive the support and encouragement of my master's thesis committee members, Susan Flader, Jeffrey Pasley, and Joanna Hearne, all of the University of Missouri–Columbia. I would also like to thank R. Lee Lyman, chair of the Department of Anthropology at the University of Missouri–Columbia, for making valuable suggestions and comments on an early version of this work.

Several librarians, archivists, and research specialists helped me navigate the collections of various institutions while I researched this book. Thank you to Bill Stolz and Christine Montgomery, both formerly of the State Historical Society of Missouri, to Kate Kiel and Linda Endersby at the Missouri State Museum, and to the staff of the special collections department of the Missouri Western State University Library for their help in steering me to many of the primary sources used in this project. I am especially indebted to David Murray of the University of Nottingham, whose scholarship pointed me to the Historical Society of Pennsylvania's collection of Mary Alicia Owen's letters. I am grateful for the assistance of Dana Dorman, a research assistant at the Historical Society of Pennsylvania, for making those letters accessible to me.

Thank you to Sandra Massey, historic preservation officer for the Sac and Fox Nation of Oklahoma, and Jimm GoodTracks, Ioway-Otoe-Missouria linguist and historian, for helping me understand the rich history of the Sac and Fox and the Ioway people. I would also like to express my appreciation to Bill McKinney, director of Parks, Recreation, and Civic Facilities for the city of St. Joseph, Missouri, for sharing his research and enthusiasm for Mary Alicia Owen with me. Lance Foster deserves a thank you as well for sharing his knowledge of both the Ioway people and the practice of hoodoo. I also appreciate the effort of the staff at the University of Missouri Press for their patient guidance.

Many thanks to my wife Chris and my daughter Tess, who have indulged me in my ramblings about Mary Alicia Owen for more than five years. Additionally, I would like to thank Chris for her comments and suggestions on this work in all of its previous versions.

VOODOO PRIESTS, NOBLE SAVAGES, AND OZARK GYPSIES

Introduction

In June 1948, workmen began to demolish an eighty-nine-year-old house hidden away in an overgrown lot at the northwest corner of Ninth and Jules Streets in St. Joseph, Missouri. Inside, the structure had already been stripped of its ornamental fireplace surrounds and the walnut newel post and spindles that had once graced the front stairway leading to the second floor. The trash that littered the floors, which included dozens of books on a variety of topics and a broken bust of the German poet, playwright, and philosopher Friedrich Schiller, hinted at the wide-reaching interests of the home's former residents. As he pried up the dining room floor, worker Archie Shull nearly fell into a large hole that had been concealed under the floorboards. The hole, it turned out, was the remains of a well, and the workers could hear water splash as they tossed books, chunks of broken plaster, and other debris into its black bottom.[1]

"Passersby look through the heavy foliage of ancient trees and conclude the city has moved on from the old Owen home at 306 North Ninth Street," the *St. Joseph News-Press* had proclaimed a few years earlier. "They are wrong; the city has not yet caught up with it. It was from this house with its half block of ground that three sisters with scientific minds moved to all parts of the world to investigate nature and write learnedly of their findings."[2]

For eight decades, the house had been a hive of activity and a hub of intellectual curiosity. In the years after the Civil War, it had been the home of James A. Owen, Agnes Cargill Owen, their five children, and their assorted household servants. Over the decades, as two of the children, Herbert Owen and Florence Owen Orr, moved out and the elderly parents passed away, it became the permanent home of three remarkable sisters, none of whom ever married. Though the women never moved away from their childhood home, their world was not one of insular confinement. There, in rooms lined with books and works of art, the three worked at careers that took them to faraway places. They entertained guests from around the world and they corresponded with some of the leading intellectuals of the day. The home, it was said, was "a Mecca for those who were interested in the better things in life."[3]

Juliette Owen, the youngest of the sisters, had been an artist and ornithologist and was also the only Owen child to live in the house her entire life. After her older sisters died, she lived at the residence with thirty-seven cats, a bantam rooster, a hen, and an unknown number of pigeons, until 1943, when she died in the same room in which she had been born eighty-four years earlier.[4] Luella Owen, more commonly known to her family and friends as Ella, was a geologist who had circled the globe and explored the depths of caves across the United States. She had been a small girl when the house was built and she too had died there. The best-known of the three sisters was Mary Alicia Owen, who lived in the house from the age of nine until her death in 1935. Within the house's walls, the eldest Owen child had written at least three books, several academic articles, and an untold number of short stories and poems.

"I don't think [the family] will either sell or rent the house where . . . [the three] sisters lived for so many years," Robert Orr, the executor of the Owen estate stated after his three great-aunts had passed away. "They won't want anyone else living there." Thus, the demolition of the Owen house served as a symbolic end to three distinguished careers. Today, a church parking lot marks the spot where the home once stood. Like the debris that lies at the bottom of the well that supplied the Owen family with water, many details about the work and the lives of the intellectual pioneers who once lived and worked there are now obscured and have been forgotten. This book attempts to unearth some details about the extraordinary life and career of one of those three sisters, Mary Alicia Owen.

Mary Owen is perhaps best known as a folklorist who studied and wrote about the culture, legends, and folkways of Missouri's African Americans. Her articles on the practice of hoodoo—or as it was often called during Owen's time, voodoo—appeared in such scholarly publications as the *Journal of American Folklore* and *The Folk-Lorist*. Her book *Old Rabbit the Voodoo and Other Sorcerers*, originally published in 1893, solidified her reputation as an expert in the field. Owen also made significant contributions to the study of American Indian culture through her work with the Meskwaki, or Sac and Fox.[5] Her 1904 book *Folk-lore of the Musquakie Indians of North America* is part folklore analysis, part anthropological investigation, and part catalogue of the more than one hundred artifacts Owen acquired from tribal members over several decades of contact with them.

This book is not the first investigation into Owen's life and work. Several authors have written about her work and pondered her legacy as a folklorist. Jean Fahey Eberle and Doris Land Mueller have both written books about the pathbreaking careers of Owen and her sisters. William McNeil and Mary Elizabeth Allcorn have examined Mary Owen's achievements in a world that was dominated by men. McNeil and Allcorn have argued that she rose above the limitations that the era placed on women to become an important contributor in the field of folklore.[6] Alison K. Brown and Neil Schmitz have offered valuable insights into Owen's role as a nonnative interpreter of American Indian culture, while David Murray and Jeffrey E. Anderson have relied on her research to launch their own investigations into the African American practice of conjure or hoodoo.[7]

Despite this attention, however, a significant portion of Mary Owen's career has been overlooked. Few recall that she also wrote poetry, fiction, and at least one play. In fact, before embarking on a career as a folklorist, Owen wrote for a St. Joseph newspaper and published several short stories and poems in popular magazines. In 1896, she published *The Daughter of Alouette*, a novel about a young woman of French and American Indian ancestry living in the ethnically mixed settlement of St. Joseph, Missouri, in the mid-nineteenth century. One of Owen's last known published works was a play, *The Sacred Council Hills*, which she printed herself in 1909. *The Sacred Council Hills* tells the story of the love that blossoms between a young Sac and Fox couple during the tribe's forced removal from the state of Missouri in 1837. Despite the fact that works of fiction constitute a substantial portion of her output, they have received scarcely more than a mention in existing investigations of her career and only one of her many short stories, "The Taming of Tarias," which appeared in 1889, has previously been identified by title.

This oversight can be attributed in part to the fact that, as no definitive bibliography of Owen's published short stories and poems is known to exist, they are not easily accessible. Even now, in the age of searchable digital archives, only a few of her early stories have been pulled from the sea of popular nineteenth-century magazines in which they first appeared. The search for her published works is further complicated by the fact that, as a young woman, Owen wrote under a pseudonym, Julia Scott. Some might justifiably argue that these works of fiction were products of the era in which they were published and have not stood up well to the test of time. Nonetheless, they warrant analysis because of what they can tell us about Owen as a person and about her later work as a folklorist. These stories, written for consumption in the popular press, can also help us to better understand Owen in the context of her time. This body of work adds depth to Owen's story and allows us to see her as versatile author with a multifaceted career. These works of fiction not only demonstrate her wit and humor, but they show that she was savvy enough to know her audience and to write fiction that satisfied their expectations.

In order to investigate the life of Mary Alicia Owen, it is necessary to begin with a close look at the St. Joseph, Missouri, of her childhood. Though the Owen family's roots reached back to Kentucky and Virginia, Mary was very much a product of this western Missouri town. St. Joseph was established just four years before her birth, and both she and the dusty trading post matured quickly amid the optimism of the boom and bust economy that characterized many western settlements in the late nineteenth century. St. Joseph's unique geographical and political history created a settlement with a highly diverse ethnic population in the middle decades of the nineteenth century. In those decades, it was possible to find significant populations of African Americans, American Indians, French Creoles, and European Americans living within a single day's horse ride of the community. To some extent, these groups came together to live, work, and trade in St. Joseph, the region's economic center. The ethnically mixed community that resulted presented Owen with the opportunity to form close associations with members of the African American and American Indian communities.

The optimism that fueled St. Joseph's early growth was interrupted by years of border violence, the bloody Civil War that followed, and the vigilante brutality that persisted in the region into the 1870s. This ongoing violence had a strong impact on Mary's personal development. Like many Southern families in St. Joseph, the Owen family suffered hardship, intimidation, and personal loss in the violence of the war years. As a result, the family became very close. During the war and long after, their lives centered on their home, where the Owen girls learned to live independently and to value and pursue their own interests.

This emphasis on self-sufficiency was reinforced when Mary traveled to New York to study at Vassar College, a school that was breaking new ground by offering young women the kind of liberal arts education that had previously only been accessible to men. After one year at Vassar College, Owen returned to St. Joseph determined to embark on a career as a writer. She chose writing in part because it offered a career path that was an acceptable endeavor for a woman of her status and it allowed her to engage her talents and intellect while she remained within the safe circle of her home and family.

Many of Owen's stories followed tried and true conventions of the popular romantic fiction of the day. Some, however, introduce the local flavor of western Missouri and St. Joseph into the formula of romance fiction. The best of these stories, "The Taming of Tarias," portrays the vibrancy of the multiethnic and economically stratified population that lived in St. Joseph, Missouri, in the mid-nineteenth century. In this story, Owen portrays the French trappers, Kentucky settlers, rugged frontier backwoodsmen, and affluent small-town businessmen who had lived in the region during her youth.

In 1889, Mary Owen initiated a correspondence with the folklorist Charles Godfrey Leland that led to a shift in her career. With Leland's encouragement, Owen realized that her long-standing interest in people and the stories they told would serve her well in a career as a folklorist. Her quest to find nearly forgotten bits of local folklore led her to St. Joseph's African American neighborhoods in search of conjurers who practiced hoodoo. While Owen had long been fascinated by the practice of hoodoo, she expressed ambivalence about the conjurers themselves. In part, this came from the fact that Owen had only known African Americans as slaves, hired hands, or domestic servants. As a white woman of means, she had never dealt with them on an equal basis. Owen was also disturbed by what she believed was the dark superstitious nature of hoodoo and by her perception that conjurers held too much power over those who believed in their practice. Both of these issues found their way into her writing about hoodoo and its practitioners.

After navigating the world of hoodoo, Owen faced the professional world of folklore. In 1891, Leland invited Owen to England to present a paper at the Second International Folklore Conference and encouraged her to compile her collection of African American hoodoo tales in a book.[8] At the time Owen encountered the discipline, folklorist were working hard to gain academic credibility, though there was disagreement regarding the best way to reach that goal. Long the domain of educated amateurs, folklorists were successfully establishing peer-reviewed outlets for scholarship, securing teaching positions in universities, and admitting a significant number of women to their ranks.

While these developments promised to bring great change to the field, most folklorists in both the United States and England were still heavily influenced by the theory of social evolution. Many academics of the day believed that African Americans and American Indians deserved special scholarly attention because they were representatives of an earlier, less-developed state of civilized man. By studying these cultures and their rituals, folklorists of the period believed, they could look back in time to find a version of their own primitive cultural ancestors.[9]

Owens' appearance in London led to the publication of her first book *Old Rabbit, the Voodoo, and Other Sorcerers* in 1893 and a certain amount of public renown. Because of her firsthand research experience with hoodoo practitioners, she sometime refereed to herself as the "White Voodoo."[10]

In the 1890s, Owen moved away from her hoodoo work and began to seriously study the American Indian people that lived just across the Missouri River from St. Joseph, the Sac and Fox. Even though she was not yet a professional folklorist when she first journeyed to their reservation, Owen established herself in the role of artifact collector and information gatherer early in her relationship with them. Her years of study found its first written outlet in the publication of her novel *The Daughter of Alouette*. In many ways, the book expanded on the world that Owen had created in her story "The Taming of Tarias," and it offers considerable insights into Owen's views about native people.

Despite the fact that she had spent a great deal of time with Indians and had devoted much energy to the study of their culture, Owen's fictional Indians conformed to the most prominent stereotypes of her day, those of the Noble Savage and the Vanishing Indian. Because these complex cultural myths were part of the cultural and academic context from which Owen sought to understand and portray American Indians, and because they appear prominently in her work, it is important to discuss the cultural origins and symbolic potency of these stereotypes.

Owen's book *Folk-lore of the Musquakie Indians of North America* provides insights into the nature of her interactions with tribal informants. The way Owen approached Sac and Fox people was influenced by her cultural assumptions about them. Her cultural biases profoundly shaped her knowledge of their cultural institutions and practices, and tempered her ability to accurately understand and authentically portray their culture.[11]

Owen thought native people could not function in modern civilized society and that their culture was in danger of disappearing forever. She believed that she possessed both a position of cultural authority and an affinity with native people that uniquely qualified her to document and preserve native culture and present it to European American society. Many of the myths and stereotypes that surface in *The Daughter of Alouette* are also present in *Folk-lore of the Musquakie Indians of North America*.

After the age of fifty, Owen began to travel less frequently. While her age, declining health, and family commitments may have contributed to her decision to cut back on travel, she was not idle in her final years. Always active in community clubs and social organizations, she began to devote more time and energy to nurturing local writers and folklorists through various storytellers' clubs and the newly formed Missouri Folklore Society. At the same time, she shifted her own investigations away from African American and American Indian folklore to the legends and stories that had been passed down from St. Joseph's earliest white settlers. This work, which was mostly published locally, had a lasting influence on the way Mary Alicia Owen is remembered in her hometown and home state today.

In the twenty-first century, Owen's legacy is related to the lore that settlers often repeated about the American Indians who lived in the region before them. In these myths, the so-called vanishing race believed that the hills around St. Joseph were the place they must go to begin their journey from this world into the afterlife. As Owen's legend of "The Road to Paradise" and related myths were repeated in books, articles, and works of art, they are merged with the facts of the removal of Indians from the state of Missouri in the 1830s. The resulting story softened the forced removal and made it appear to be a natural and inevitable part of the region's development. The "Road to Paradise" became a metaphor for the journey that Indians were forced to make across the Missouri River to reservations in what is now Kansas.

Owen was a complex woman whose life and work were rife with contradictions. She was a woman of keen intellect who pursued a variety of interests and who was influenced by many ideas, theories, and concepts. While some of the ideas that motivated her are timeless, many were very much associated with the era in which she lived and worked. For this reason, in the telling Owen's story, it is necessary to discuss larger stories related to the social paradigms and cultural ideas that were prevalent in her time. Ideas such as the theory of social evolution, stereotypes like those of the Noble Savage and the Vanishing Indian, and the ideological tug of war between literary and anthropological folklorists did not overly concern Owen, who claimed to dislike theories. But these ideas, and many others, did govern the way in which people of her era viewed the world, and they made an impact in Owen's writings. Clearly, this work is not the last word in the life of this extraordinary woman, but it puts forth new facts and offers new insights that are intended to give the reader the most complete portrait of Mary Alicia Owen that we have to date.

One

The Queen City of the West, 1850–1860

The life of Mary Alicia Owen is inextricably linked to the town in which she lived all of her eighty-five years, St. Joseph, Missouri. Owen's mother, Agnes Cargill, and father, James Owen, arrived in St. Joseph while the village was still in its infancy. Mary, their oldest child, was born there in 1850, just six years after the town was founded. Over her lifetime, she came to know intimately the hills that surrounded the town and the river that flowed beside it. She knew the cycle of the seasons in the Missouri River valley and the harsh extremes of its frigid winters and sweltering summers. She was familiar with the shapes and the scents of the old elms and lindens that grew in her yard and marveled at the vivid colors of the bluebirds and the croak of the rain crows that thrived there.[1]

Yet while St. Joseph was a constant in her long life, it was one that was ever changing and expanding. The small dusty village of Owen's childhood grew into the rowdy boomtown of her youth and, later, the established commercial and financial center of her adult years. In some ways, Mary Alicia Owen was more constant than the city. As St. Joseph grew and evolved, she continued to live in her childhood home, recording tales based on her memories of the city's early days. She was ever on the lookout for stories, songs, artifacts, and bits of folklore that she feared were in danger of disappearing along with the city's first log buildings and old settlers. While Owen was firmly established as a member of the St. Joseph's upper echelon, she befriended many of the minstrels, conjurers, gypsies, Ioways, Sacs, Foxes, and Kickapoos that could be found in the city's less desirable neighborhoods, on nearby reservations, and in small villages outside the city limits. She peppered these acquaintances with questions about their customs, beliefs, and favorite stories, and often bought clothing, ceremonial items, and bits of handiwork from them. The information she gained in these relationships fueled her long career as a journalist, novelist, short story writer, and folklorist. In her work, Owen also drew on her deep roots in the Blacksnake Hills and her exhaustive knowledge of the region's mythic and colorful past. Because Owen's long life and career were so closely bound to this place, it is important to begin this examination with a look at the town that was her home for over eight decades.

A dozen years prior to Mary Alicia Owen's birth, the future site of St. Joseph consisted of little more than a trading post run by a lively character about whom Owen would write more than once, Joseph Robidoux Jr. Robidoux's father, who was also a trader, had come from Montreal and settled in St. Louis by way of Kaskaskia in what is now the state of Illinois. Born in St. Louis in 1783, the younger Robidoux worked alongside his father in the fur trade. A tall, heavy-set man with dark piercing eyes and a swarthy complexion, Robidoux joined his brothers Antoine, Francis, Isadore, and Michel to trade at Council Bluff in 1809. Council Bluff, located along the Missouri River near the present-day town of Fort Calhoun, Nebraska, was the spot where Lewis and Clark's Corps of Discovery famously held their meeting with members of the Otoe nation in 1804. Its location near the confluence of the Missouri, Platte, and Boyer Rivers made it an ideal spot from which to conduct trade with the Otoe, Pawnee, Omaha, Ponca, and other Indian nations that lived and hunted in what are now the states of Nebraska, Missouri, and Iowa.

Robidoux and his brothers operated the post for more than a dozen tumultuous years. Their business dealings often led to personal disputes. One of Robidoux's most contentious relationships was with Manuel Lisa, a trader of Spanish ancestry who operated a competing post nearby. The two were fierce competitors whose desire to outdo one another in business apparently knew no bounds. On one occasion, Robidoux was said to have locked Lisa in a storage cellar in order to complete a transaction with some Pawnee traders without interference. Given this kind of behavior, it is not surprising that

St. Joseph, Missouri, c. 1850. This etching depicts a romanticized view of the village of St. Joseph at about the time that Mary Alicia Owen was born. The Missouri River, shown in the upper left, would prove to be a valuable asset that helped make the small town an important trading center. (Courtesy of the State Historical Society of Missouri, Columbia)

Robidoux and his brothers often found themselves in legal trouble. Between 1809 and 1822, the five were named in no fewer than thirty court cases in the St. Louis circuit court and court of common pleas. In these cases, the Robidouxs were either accused or accused others of such crimes as breach of contract and failure to pay debts.[2]

Robidoux's business relationship with the Chouteau family of St. Louis also became an ongoing source of conflict. Though he was an employee of a company owned by the Chouteaus, Robidoux was engaged in a number of his own trade deals on the side. He was licensed to trade under the name Robidoux and Company as early as 1817. On August 16, 1826, he received a license to trade near Bellevue, a site just a few miles south of Council Bluff in present-day Nebraska. Two years later, in August 1828, Robidoux and a partner named Baptiste Roy received a license to trade at the Blacksnake Hills as well, though they did not establish a post there at that time. The Chouteaus believed that Robidoux's moonlighting cut deeply into their own profits, and in October 1828 they bought out the trader's stock and paid him a thousand dollars to quit the business altogether and leave the area for three years. During his time away from the fur trade, Robidoux returned to St. Louis where he worked as a confectioner and baker.[3]

After the three-year period ended, in about 1830 or 1831, Robidoux established a trading post in the Blacksnake Hills. This time he was an employee of the American Fur Company and collected a salary of eighteen hundred dollars a year. The Blacksnake Hills, located on a bend in the river near open bottomland known as St. Michael's Prairie, were a distinctive feature of the Missouri River valley. During a trip up the Missouri River in 1833, the German prince Maximilian von Wied described the hills as "moderate eminences, with many singular forms, [and] an alternation of wooded and open green spots." It was on one of these open green spots, near the point at which Blacksnake Creek entered the Missouri River, that Robidoux built a cabin and a trading house. Business at the post proved to be lucrative, and by the time Maximilian returned during his trip downriver in 1834, Robidoux had purchased it from the American Fur Company and had become an independent trader.[4]

Robidoux's success came in no small part from his post's location at a crossroads of frontier commerce and cultures. For more than a century, the fur trade along the Missouri River had brought together traders, many of whom were French like Robidoux, with people from American Indian nations such as the Ioway, Potawatomi, Sac, and Fox. It was not uncommon for French traders who conducted business with these tribes to take up residence in Indian villages for extended periods of time. Not surprisingly, these traders often adopted the lifestyle, language, and habits of their hosts and they sometimes married Indian women. These marriages were often more than mere personal relationships, as traders and native leaders found that marriage offered them the opportunity to create advantageous business partnerships. The arrangement helped ensure that both Indians and traders received favorable treatment from business partners they knew and trusted and to whom they were linked by family bonds. Joseph Robidoux forged such bonds with native communities, and he is said to have fathered several children with American Indian women. One of his Ioway daughters, Mary, became the wife of the Ioway headman

Francis White Cloud and was the mother of longtime Ioway leader James White Cloud.[5]

In 1836, the state of Missouri annexed the Blacksnake Hills in
a deal that was known as the Platte Purchase. That year, the U.S.
government signed treaties with the Ioway, Sac and Fox, Otoe-
Missouria, Omaha, Yankton Sioux, and Santee Sioux that gave the
state a triangular-shaped piece of land that was called the Platte
country, after the river that ran through its center. The area, total-
ing more than 3,000 square miles, was located between Missouri's
original western border and the Missouri River and makes up the
present-day counties of Platte, Andrew, Buchanan, Holt, Atchison,
and Nodaway.[6] To open the way for white settlers to legally move
into the Platte country, the treaty dictated the removal of all Indians to reservations on the west side of the Missouri River. Settlers
had been squatting illegally in the region for years, but after the
ratification of the Platte Purchase, greater numbers of whites were
attracted by the opportunity to claim land.

After the organization of Buchanan County, in 1839, Joseph Robidoux had hoped that the U.S. government would reward his efforts to maintain peaceful relations with the indigenous population
around the Blacksnake Hills by granting him two square miles of
land. The government failed to make such an offer and he filed a
claim for one half section, or 320 acres, of land near the trading post.
By that time, a few families had built cabins in the vicinity of the
post and interest in platting a town on the site began to grow. In the
fall of 1839, investors from Independence, Missouri, nearly closed
a deal with Robidoux to purchase his land with the intention of di-
viding it into town lots. Legend has it that after an argument over
a game of cards, the trader angrily backed out of the deal and the
investors returned home empty-handed.[7]

As settlers continued to move into the Blacksnake Hills, the region's economy became less dependent on the fur trade and more
reliant on various kinds of agriculture. Accordingly, Robidoux altered
his business strategy. While he operated a ferry to maintain trade
with the Indians west of the Missouri River, he also opened a flour
mill, a hemp warehouse, and a tobacco warehouse to serve the needs
of local farmers. Other businessmen soon established other enterprises, including a sawmill, tavern, blacksmith shop, cabinet shop,

brick kiln, and other enterprises necessary to supply the growing community. By 1840 the settlement had its first post office, which was operated by Robidoux's son Jules. As the settlement's population reached 200, Robidoux saw that the time to establish a town was at hand. In June 1843 he asked two surveyors, F. W. Smith and Simeon Kemper, each to draw up plans for the new town. Robidoux chose Smith's plan over Kemper's because it featured narrower streets and larger town lots, favoring the larger lots because he could sell them for more money. In July, he traveled to St. Louis to file Smith's survey and to legally transform the settlement at Blacksnake Hills into the town of St. Joseph. The new town was named for Robidioux's patron saint, and the original plat included streets named for his wife Angelique and his children Faraon, Jules, Francis, Felix, Edmund, Charles, and Sylvanie. According to Rudolph Kurz, a Swiss artist who visited St. Joseph in the late 1840s, Robidoux initially sold town lots measuring 40 feet by 140 feet for ten dollars or, if purchasers were short on cash, one yoke of oxen. By 1848, the lots had tripled in value and by 1850 they sold for as much as $600.[8]

Just three months after St. Joseph's founding, Mary Alicia Owen's grandparents, James and Agnes Gilmore Crookes Cargill, arrived at the town's river landing located at the foot of Francis Street. According to legend, Joseph Robidoux braved a miserable September rainstorm to personally welcome the entourage, which included the Cargill's four grown children, one son-in-law, and two slaves, to his new settlement. Prior to his arrival in Missouri, James Cargill had twice resettled his family to start new business ventures. Born in Liberty, Maine, in 1789, Cargill moved to Pittsburg, Pennsylvania, as a young man in 1812. He married Belfast, Maine, native Agnes Crookes, who was also known as Nancy, in 1814. The couple had four children, John, George, Abigail, and Agnes. The Cargills remained in Pittsburg for several years while James was involved in lumber and shipping operations. In 1829 the family moved to the town of Wheeling, in what was then part of Virginia, where James operated a supply company that outfitted emigrants traveling west to Kentucky and Tennessee. The business proved profitable until he and a partner suffered heavy losses in the financial panic of 1838–1839. After struggling to repay his creditors, Cargill once again cast his eye to the West in search of new opportunities.[9]

In early 1843, Cargill and his son John spent several weeks in the Missouri River valley looking for a place to resettle. After exploring the region around the Blacksnake Hills, the two decided that St. Joseph was a prime spot from which to launch their next ventures. They returned to Virginia to prepare the family for a journey that would take them westward on the Ohio, Mississippi, and Missouri Rivers to their new home. At least one member of the family did not share their enthusiasm for the new settlement. Seeing St. Joseph's rain-soaked streets for the first time, the Cargill's twenty-four-year-old daughter Abigail cried and begged to be taken back to Wheeling. As the town's housing had not kept pace with its growing population, the Cargills found that there were no accommodations for them. For a short time, they remained in their cabins aboard the *Lexington*, the steamer upon which they had traveled up the Missouri River. Meanwhile Joseph Robidoux evicted a boarder and offered the Cargills the newly vacated room in his home. The Cargill family remained under Robidoux's roof until their new house at Burr Oak, a farmstead they purchased east of town, could be constructed. Despite his varied business interests, James Cargill was listed as a farmer in the 1850 U.S. Census. With the help of his son George and a handful of slaves, he grew hemp, wheat, corn, fruit, and vegetables at the farmstead. By 1860, the farm was yielding 300 bushels of oats, 3,000 bushels of wheat, and eight tons of hay annually on 100 acres of land. The Cargills kept sixty hogs and thirty sheep and owned horses, mules, and oxen.[10]

In 1847, four years after the Cargills settled in St. Joseph, Mary Alicia Owen's father, James Alfred Owen, arrived in the town, which by then had grown to a thousand people. A native of Louisville, Kentucky, Owen had grown up in meager surroundings after the early death of his father, Nelson Reid Owen. When James Owen was sixteen, his mother, Nancy Baber Owen, remarried, and a year later young Owen left home to study law with Louisville judge James I. Dozier. After completing his studies, Owen left Kentucky in 1846 to join his uncles John Owen and Ignatius Owen in Missouri. He taught school in Platte City, Missouri, for a year and on May 19, 1847, he moved to St. Joseph. There, Owen studied law with Judge Solomon L. Leonard and was admitted to the Missouri bar in 1848. Less than a year after settling in St. Joseph, Owen established a law practice and became engaged to James Cargill's youngest daughter,

Agnes Jeanette, whom he married on August 3, 1848. After the wedding, Owen entered into a business partnership with his father-in-law but retained his law practice.[11]

As James Owen and James Cargill established themselves in their homes and in commerce, the city of St. Joseph grew quickly around them. The late 1840s were boom years for the new community as settlers traveling on the Oregon Trail discovered that they could shave 100 miles from their journey by fording the Missouri River at St. Joseph rather than farther south at the town of Independence. The discovery channeled thousands of travelers and an infusion of money into the once-sleepy river town. Traffic on the trail accelerated after a mill foreman named James Marshall discovered traces of gold in a stream near John Sutter's mill in California's central valley in January 1848. Just over a year after the discovery, more than 2,500 wagons crossed the Missouri River in the St. Joseph area in a ten-week period with an estimated total of 50,000 people passing through the city in the year of 1849. The gold rush and the boom that accompanied it pushed St. Joseph's population from 200 in 1843 to nearly 3,500 in 1850.[12]

On February 6, 1849, the *St. Joseph Gazette* described a bustling city that bore little resemblance to the small trading post that had occupied the site just a decade earlier.

> St. Joseph contains a population of 1,800. Nineteen stores are now in successful operation, with an aggregate stock of goods for the year 1848, of from $250,000 to $300,000. Three new large stores will be opened in the present season, which will increase the stock for the year 1849, to $350,000 to $400,000. In addition to the above there are in town two flouring mills, two steam saw mills, nine blacksmith shops, four wagon shops, two extensive sheet iron ware manufactories, two large saddleries and harness making establishments, etc.[13]

To secure the town's future growth, a group of boosters, which included Joseph Robidoux and state senator Robert Stewart, led a campaign to make St. Joseph the western terminus of a proposed 200-mile trans-Missouri railroad. With Stewart's help, the Missouri general assembly chartered the Hannibal and St. Joseph Rail Road in February 1847.[14] Though it would be twelve years before the railroad connected the city to commercial hubs like Chicago and St. Louis, enthusiasm for the project led one booster to optimistically proclaim in 1850 that it "requires no uncommon degree of sagacity to foresee the influence [St. Joseph] is one day destined to wield . . . in the future chronicles of the west."[15]

During its early history, St. Joseph's growing population was highly diverse. As European American settlers flooded into the Platte region, they joined the French traders and American Indian people who had occupied the region before the city was founded. Even after the Ioway, Lenni Lenape, Potawatomi, Kickapoo, and Sac and Fox nations were removed to the west side of the Missouri River in 1837, many Indians continued to visit St. Joseph to trade. The Swiss-born artist Rudolph Friedrich Kurz traveled to St. Joseph in 1848 in the hope of sketching and painting pictures of Indians from life. In his journal, Kurz reported that he was not disappointed. "Even during the first month of my stay in St. Joseph I had chances every day to study Indians that came in bands from different neighboring tribes. . . . They came to St. Joseph to make their purchases, because they could supply their needs there at more reasonable rates than with the traders."[16]

The region was also home to a sizable African American population. Like many counties along the Missouri River, Buchanan County, in which the city of St. Joseph is located, had been settled by many people who, like the Owens and Cargills, had Southern ties. Many of these settlers brought the agricultural traditions of tobacco and hemp farming with them. These labor-intensive crops relied heavily on slaves, and it is estimated that on the eve of the Civil War there were 2,000 slaves living in Buchanan County. Of those, some 600 lived in St. Joseph. Most of the slaves who lived inside the city limits worked as domestic servants, and slaves worked in the homes of the Cargill and Owen families in the years before the Civil War.[17] Though they were northerners by birth, James and Agnes Cargill had owned several slaves when they lived in Virginia. While they sold most of them before moving to Missouri, they did bring two slaves with them. Shortly after arriving in St. Joseph, the Cargills bought two more slaves in the nearby town of Savannah, Missouri. "Aunt Mary" and "Uncle Adam" were a married couple that cost the Cargills $2,200. Mary worked as a cook in the home and Adam was a farm hand. By 1850, the Cargills owned six slaves: two adult women, two adult men, and two children under the age of five. A decade later, there were four adult slaves in the Cargill household and one fourteen-year-old girl working in the Owen home.[18]

There is anecdotal evidence that American Indians and African Americans in the St. Joseph region interacted socially and that some intermarried. While connections between these two socially marginalized groups in Missouri have not been well documented, they were sometimes brought together by the institution of slavery. In the antebellum South, members of some Indian nations, such as the Cherokee, owned African American slaves. While this practice was not common in Missouri, the state did once allow both Indians and African Americans to be kept as slaves. The enslavement of indigenous people in Missouri dates back to the Spanish colonial period. Although the Spanish emancipated Indian slaves in the 1780s, the practice continued clandestinely until it was stuck down in court in 1836.[19]

In some cases, Indian communities outside the state of Missouri provided safe harbor for fugitive slaves. Historian Robert J. Willoughby has written that once they reached the western banks of the Missouri River, runaway slaves found refuge among the Indians who lived in what are now the states of Kansas and Oklahoma. Some used Indian reservations as places to lay over on their journey to the northern free states while others apparently stayed long enough to intermarry with tribal members. There is evidence that the Ioway nation, who have occupied a reservation 40 miles northwest of St. Joseph near the town of White Cloud, Kansas, since 1837, allowed African Americans to live with them. At a council with Ioway leaders on April 14, 1846, Superintendant of Indian Affairs in St. Louis Thomas Harvey expelled at least one African American, translator Jeffery Deroine (also known as Dorion) from the Ioway's reservation.

"This is your country," Harvey told the Ioway leader Francis White Cloud. "You are Red Birds. Black Birds have no business among you. I will therefore send the Black Birds away. You must now think how this country was reserved for Indians not Negroes. I can not permit them to associate with my red children." While Harvey was speaking primarily about Deroine, the fact that he used the plural throughout his statement leaves open the possibility that he meant to expel other African Americans from the reservation as well.[20]

In her first book, *Old Rabbit, the Voodoo, and Other Sorcerers,* published in 1893, Mary Alicia Owen wrote about slave women who come from mixed African American and American Indian backgrounds. In *Old Rabbit,* Owen portrays herself as Tow Head, a precocious and stubborn young girl from a well-to-do white family. Young Tow Head takes every opportunity to escape the strict confines of "the folks up at The House" in order to keep company with five slave women who meet to smoke and tell stories in the cabin of Granny, a woman of African American and Lenni Lenape heritage. Granny's circle of friends included Madame Angelique Bougareau, also known as Big Angy, whom Owen describes as a gardener and businesswoman whose parents were a French hunter and the daughter of a chief of the Ioway nation. Another of the women, Aunt Em'ly, came from an African American mother and a father who was a member of the Fox nation, while Aunt Mary was described as being part African American and part "Injun." The fifth member of Granny's circle of friends was a woman Owen called Aunt Mymee Whitehead, the only member of the group who did not have American Indian ancestors. She was born in the African nation of Guinea and was brought to Kentucky with her mother while she was still a child. When Whitehead was ten or twelve years old, she and her mother were brought to Missouri.[21]

Owen spoke at some length about Whitehead in an 1891 lecture she delivered at the Second International Folklore Congress in London. In the lecture, Owen recalled that she had been fascinated by the fact that Whitehead, who was her nurse, was a conjurer. Conjure is the African American folk practice of enlisting help from the spirit world to accomplish practical goals through spells or potions. Historian Jeffrey E. Anderson has defined a conjurer "as a professional magic practitioner who typically receives payment in return for his or her goods and services." Conjure, or hoodoo as it is sometimes called, has roots in Africa but has been heavily influenced by European and American Indian cultural traditions. Conjure was commonly practiced by African Americans in Missouri and elsewhere in the American South during the mid- and late nineteenth century.

While it is difficult to know the degree of artistic license Owen employed when writing *Old Rabbit,* it appears that her portraits of Mymee Whitehead and Aunt Mary were based on actual residents of St. Joseph. Whitehead appears in both *Old Rabbit* and in

Owen's 1891 lecture, where she is listed as an important consultant in Owen's research into hoodoo or, as Owen called it, voodoo. It is possible that the Aunt Mary who appears in *Old Rabbit* is the same woman who came to the Cargill household from Savannah, Missouri, with her husband Adam. Because slave records included in the 1850 census do not list the Cargills' slaves by name, there is no way to verify that either one of the women worked in the household or belonged to the family. Nonetheless, Owen's recollections about young Tow Head, Mymee Whitehead, Aunt Mary, and their friends who gathered in the cabin provide us with a rare glimpse into the fluid racial boundaries that characterized a portion of St. Joseph's population in the mid-nineteenth century

Amid St. Joseph's economic growth in the decade before the Civil War, the Owen family also prospered and grew. By 1860, James and Agnes Owen had four daughters, Mary Alicia (who was born in 1850), Luella Agnes (born in 1852), Florence Alma (born about 1855), and Juliette Amelia (born in 1859), and one son, Herbert Alfred (born in 1857).[22] Two other sons either died in childbirth or as infants. The Owen family was among the first to join Christ Episcopal Church, which the Cargills had helped establish in about 1852.[23]

Duties outside the household often kept James Owen away from his young family in the 1850s. As a lawyer, he was sometimes away from home for extended periods, riding the circuit of northwest Missouri county courthouses on horseback. Later, politics occupied much of Owen's time while he served as St. Joseph's city assessor from 1853 to 1854 and again between 1857 and 1859. In the early 1850s, Owen was also involved in a business partnership with his father-in-law. Operating under the name James Cargill and Company, the partnership owned the Eagle Mill, a steam-powered gristmill said to have been the largest of its kind west of St. Louis. Cargill and Company sold flour locally and to travelers who stopped in St. Joseph to take on supplies for the journey west on the Oregon Trail. The partners also supplied flour to at least one business that traded with Indians at an agency at Bellevue, located south of Omaha, Nebraska. Jean Fahey Eberle has written that the partnership between Owen and Cargill was ill-fated and that the two strong-willed men rarely saw eye to eye. In 1852, a rumor was circulated in St. Joseph alleging that Owen had tried to hit his father-in-law with a club during an argument. According to Eberle, Owen blamed

Cargill for initiating the rumor, which he claimed was false. Though Owen demanded that Cargill publicly denounce the falsehood, he apparently did not. The two men reportedly never spoke again and relations between the two families became permanently strained.[24]

If such tensions did exist, they would have been exacerbated by the fact that the Owen family had lived under the Cargill's roof in the early 1850s. James, Agnes, and Mary Owen were listed as part of the Cargill household in the 1850 census. At the time, the value of Owen's real estate holdings was a mere fraction of those held by his father-in-law, so the arrangement may have been one of financial necessity. It is unclear how long the Owens lived in the Cargill's home, or if they lived for a time in another of the various properties that the Cargills owned. At the time of James Cargill's death in 1858, he and his wife owned eight town lots in St. Joseph and 400 acres of land outside the city limits.

A year after Cargill's death, the Owen family moved into a new home northeast of St. Joseph's business district. Situated on two spacious lots located on the northwest corner of Ninth and Jules Streets, the home was a two-story, clapboard Italianate structure with a T-shaped floor plan. The formal entrance to the house faced east, toward Ninth Street, and an open two-story porch stretched across the south side of the house's rear ell. Because the house sat on a rise that sloped away to the south, the Owen family would have enjoyed a vista that allowed them to watch St. Joseph's downtown expand toward the east over the decades that they lived there.[25]

After settling in his new home, James Owen initiated a drawn-out battle with his in-laws over James Cargill's estate. In 1862, he sued his brother-in-law Erastus Ford, husband of Abigail Cargill Ford, alleging that Ford had harvested five thousand dollars' worth of lumber from property that Agnes Cargill Owen was due to inherit from her parents. Owen demanded that Ford desist from cutting the wood and asked him for six thousand dollars in damages. When Agnes Cargill and Abigail Cargill Ford refused to join Owen in the suit, he added them to the list of defendants. The case moved slowly through the courts, hampered no doubt by the disruption of the Civil War. Finally, in 1872 the case was heard in the Missouri Supreme Court, which ruled against Owen. Though the verdict was no doubt disappointing for Owen, the decade-long feud certainly must have taken its toll on both sides of the extended family. From documents filed in the proceedings, it is clear that James Owen and Erastus Ford held feelings of visceral mistrust, jealousy, and hatred toward one another. In an accusation meant, no doubt, to injure Ford's pride, Owen alleged that his brother-in-law stole the wood because he was financially destitute and needed money. Ford countered by insinuating that James Owen was siphoning off the riches of the Cargill family for his own benefit. Ford further charged that Owen had defrauded John Cargill out of 180 acres of land that Cargill was set to inherit from his father.[26]

Family feuding aside, the fact remains that on the eve of the Civil War, the Owen and the Cargill families were prominent in St. Joseph's business, religious, political, and social circles. However, as the storm cloud of war gathered across the United States, the prominence of the two families would be challenged by a broader, more brutal conflict. Living in St. Joseph, the Owens and Cargills were aware of the danger long before the war started, as violence spread throughout the Kansas-Missouri border region. As Southern sympathizers, they would suffer at the hands of Radical Republicans long after the fighting ceased. Like many Missourians, even those who were not directly involved in military fighting, they would be drawn into the conflict and would suffer its ramifications for decades to come.

Two

"Our Unhappy Country," 1860–1870

Even though war loomed on the horizon, the Owen family had reason to be optimistic as the decade of the 1860s began. From the vantage point of their new home on Ninth Street, they were no doubt aware that, the fighting over slavery and state's rights notwithstanding, St. Joseph continued to grow and prosper. The discovery of gold near Pike's Peak in 1859 had brought a second wave of travelers through the community along the Oregon Trail. This increased traffic was enhanced by the completion of the Hannibal and St. Joseph Railroad and the arrival of the first passenger train on Valentine's Day, 1859. By becoming the western terminus of the railroad, St. Joseph had successfully fended off competition from the newer and smaller community of Kansas City to remain western Missouri's most prominent business hub and an important way station for goods and people moving west.

With its link to the commercial centers of the East secured via the railroad, St. Joseph turned its attention to opening trade with the ever-expanding West. To this end, hundreds gathered at the Patee House Hotel on April 3, 1860, to watch the inaugural run of a new postal delivery venture called the Pony Express. Using a chain of riders, the Pony Express promised to transport letters approximately 1,900 miles between St. Joseph and Sacramento, California, in just ten days. By extending the reach of the railroad and the telegraph, the Pony Express made it possible to send mail from coast to coast, through St. Joseph, with unprecedented speed. Speaking at the ceremony marking the first express rider's departure from the Patee

House, St. Joseph mayor M. Jeff Thompson expressed his hope that, as transportation and communication with the West improved, the city would retain its position as the gateway through which much westward traffic passed.[1]

James Owen, no doubt, calculated the ways in which the railroad and the Pony Express might contribute to the prosperity of his business interests and to the vitality of his community. In 1860, St. Joseph's population had reached nearly 9,000. In the next year it would grow to 11,000. The city now had a professional police force of one marshal, one deputy, and six officers. For those less affluent than the Owen family, the city opened its first public school. Had it not been for the uncertainty of war, the future of St. Joseph and the Owen family would have seemed bright.[2] From his office at Second and Jules, James Owen continued to practice law and rent various properties that he owned, which by his own account were valued at $50,000, or about $1.1 million in today's dollars.

But the good times in St. Joseph and in the Owen household deteriorated rapidly. Just over a year after the first Pony Express rider galloped west from the Patee House, James Owen was writing about the ways the war was having a negative impact on his business and on life in St. Joseph:

> This has been the most eventful year in my recollection. The South Carolinians fired on Fort Sumter in April and the long dreaded crisis arrived. Hopes sunk—war and arms—enlistments —government contracts—scrip—bonds—spoliations—plunder —confiscation and robbery. . . . The Revolution promises little more than destruction. It is controlled by maddened factions which daily grow more violent. The precipice may be just ahead.[3]

Many who had been paying attention to the region's political climate had been expecting violence and mayhem for at least half of the decade prior to the attack on Fort Sumter. In 1854, the Kansas-Nebraska Act had created the new territory of Kansas directly across the Missouri River from St. Joseph. The act allowed the residents of Kansas to decide for themselves whether they would become a slave state or a free state. The territory immediately became a violent battleground upon which the national debate over the future of slavery in the United States was fought. Afraid that Kansas would be overrun by abolitionists, pro-slavery Missourians monitored their western border, questioning incoming settlers on where they stood on the slave issue and then terrorizing those who stated their allegiance to the free-state cause. When a Kansas vote to elect members of the territorial legislature took place in March 1855, so many Missouri "border ruffians" crossed into the territory to cast ballots and intimidate free-state supporters from voting that the election went in favor of the pro-slavery bloc. This blatant display of election fraud infuriated abolitionists such as John Brown, whose efforts to make Kansas a free territory led him and a small group of followers to murder five men along Pottawatomie Creek in Kansas in 1856. The violence that consumed the Missouri-Kansas border in those years earned the new territory the name "bleeding Kansas."

While the border war of the 1850s brought the threat of violence to the region about 100 miles south of St. Joseph, the outbreak of Civil War in 1861 introduced intimidation, brutality, and terror into the city's streets. Given the large number of slaves living in the city, it is no surprise that many residents held strong pro-Southern sympathies at the outbreak of the war. These sentiments led to a display of anti-Union sentiment on the roof of the St. Joseph post office in May 1861. Postmaster John L. Bittinger, appointed by the Republican administration of newly elected President Abraham Lincoln, refused to heed requests from Southern sympathizers to remove the United States flag from its place on top of the building. Finally, a group of men led by a reportedly inebriated M. Jeff Thompson, who by that time had exchanged his duties as mayor for those of a colonel in the pro-Southern Missouri State Guard, climbed to the top of the post office, ripped the flag to pieces, and replaced it with a Confederate flag as a crowd of supporters watched from the street. The incident, which was widely reported in the press, brought St. Joseph's Southern sympathies to the attention of the nation. Thompson quickly fled St. Joseph, and within a month, Federal troops arrived from Fort Leavenworth to begin an occupation that would last until the war's end.[4]

Like other citizens across Missouri, most denizens of St. Joseph had preferred that the state remain in the Union. The state's pro-Southern governor, Claiborne Fox Jackson, advocated secession, however. After attempts to reach a compromise with leaders of the federal government failed, and federal troops led by Nathaniel Lyon moved toward Jefferson City, Jackson abandoned the state capital and fled in June 1861 with members of the state guard. In Jackson's absence, the federal government established a pro-Union provisional government as General Lyon pursued the governor and the forces under his command. Some of the first battles of the American Civil War took place in the Missouri towns of Boonville, Carthage, and Springfield as federal armed forces succeeded in pushing Jackson and his troops into Arkansas. Lyon died in the Battle of Wilson's Creek just south of Springfield.

While Confederate regular troops were largely absent from Missouri by early 1862, armed guerrilla units, often known as bushwhackers, roamed the state terrorizing, robbing, and killing Union sympathizers for the remainder of the war. In response, pro-Union bands of Jayhawkers crossed the Missouri border from Kansas to exact revenge on citizens they suspected of being Southern sympathizers. The confession of a twenty-year-old Jayhawker from Carroll County, Missouri, named Jesse Stovall shows how such bands operated. In a deposition given to the provost marshal's office in Chillicothe in December 1863, Stovall recounted how what had started out to be a Jayhawker campaign against slavery and slaveholders soon turned into a rampage of random violence. "When I joined the Red Legs in Kansas . . . ," Stovall stated, "the general understanding among that band was to take all that rebels had from them, but the general practice was to take whatever suited them from any body living in Missouri." In his confession, Stovall admitted to participating in at least one hanging, to burning homes and other buildings, and to stealing money, household goods, and livestock.[5]

In an effort to control this rampant violence, federal troops tightened their grip on cities like St. Joseph that they perceived to be Confederate strongholds. The federal soldiers that arrived in the city in May 1861 soon entrenched themselves on top of Prospect Hill, a prominent bluff located along the Missouri River just north of downtown St. Joseph. The bluff-top bastion, which the federals called Fort Smith, became a highly visible daily reminder of the fact that St. Joseph was under martial law. Every facet of life was affected by the clampdown on citizens and businesses. A curfew imposed on the city directed all people to be home by ten o'clock in the evening. To lessen the temptation to ignore the curfew, saloons and gaming houses were ordered to close at that hour as well. Later, the Union prohibited the shipping of items such as "Pork, Bacon, Hams, Beef cured or dried, Flour, Crackers, Beans, Coffee, Tea, Sugar, Salt, Molasses," and moved the hour of business closure up to six o'clock.[6]

By the fall of 1861, nearly the entire state of Missouri was under martial law. To restrict the movements of Southern sympathizers, the Union's provost marshal's office required anyone who desired to travel around the state to carry a proper military pass. Citizens who were suspected of not being loyal to the federal government were barred from travel, and only those who took an oath of loyalty were eligible to receive military passes. Under martial law, Union officials also attempted to tax Southern sympathizers, often referred to as "disloyal" citizens, for damages and death caused by rebel troops or guerrilla units. Enacted by General John Schofield, commanding officer of the Union Army's Division of Missouri, "General Order No. 3" created a system whereby disloyal citizens were forced to compensate loyal citizens for damages that Confederates caused in their county. If the citizens refused to pay the charges levied against them by Union officials, their property was seized and sold. The order stipulated that disloyal citizens would be charged $2,000 for each Union soldier or citizen killed by Confederate troops or bushwhackers in their county. Each wounded Union soldier or citizen was to be compensated $5,000 while the owners of materials that were destroyed or stolen in Confederate raids were to be paid the full replacement value of their losses. Though the order proved difficult to implement and ultimately failed, it showed how diligent Union officials could be in trying to force disloyal citizens to pay for the destruction of the war.[7]

James Owen noted that the Union troops that were sent to protect Missouri citizens from bushwhackers and Jayhawkers sometimes allowed their military zeal to turn into vigilante violence, which occasionally became as destructive as the mayhem that they had been charged with preventing. In 1862, Owen wrote, "[Colonel William R.] Penick's [Union Cavalry] Regiment was disbanded early in the year on account of the thieving propensities of his men. They then scattered through the counties of Andrew, Holt, and Nodaway and began to murder and burn. About thirty of the best citizens of Andrew County were murdered and as many houses burned in a few days. Robbery was universal. The theft of horses and mules was common."[8]

In the same entry, Owen decried the Union's failure to keep Kansas Jayhawkers from preying upon the citizens of Missouri.

> Kansas was always nourished by the Republican party, and when our unhappy country fell under this control, it became the especial object of the rulers of the nation to foster, organize and encourage an assemblage of law defying people. The War began by disarming the people of Missouri and then turning loose upon her the armed thieves and ruffians of a dozen states, but especially of Kansas, who plundered her of Eight Million Dollars worth of slaves, of horses, cattle and everything moveable, and by murdering her citizens, burning their homes, imprisoning thousands, and driving tens of thousands into exile. Hundreds of persons in Kansas became rich by plundering the helpless people of Missouri.[9]

During this reign of terror, there was no such thing as neutrality for the people of Missouri. Aware that they could be arrested, jailed, or singled out for violence because of their allegiances—or perceived allegiances—ordinary people learned to be suspicious of all but their closest friends and allies. With their Southern background, the slave-holding Owen and Cargill families were among those who were well-known to support the Confederate cause. Though none of the men in either family served in the military, they too were pushed into action during the Civil War.

Several members of both the Cargill and Owen families were caught in the blockade set up by the provost marshal's office. Mary Alicia Owen's uncles, John and George Cargill, were suspected of helping a local Confederate captain named Reuben Kay escape St. Joseph for safety in the South. Because the Cargill brothers were implicated in the incident, Union sympathizers burned the family business, Eagle Mill. John Cargill was jailed and the family's farm, Burr Oak, was looted of furniture and livestock. George Cargill fled St. Joseph to avoid an angry mob that wanted to hang him. Mary Alicia Owen's grandmother, Agnes Cargill, was given a military pass and allowed to travel to West Virginia, where she remained until the war ended.[10]

Meanwhile James Owen wrote in 1862 that Union soldiers "have frequently arrested me and I have been ordered to report to the Guard house. The object of the Dutch and Yankee abolitionists is to drive me away and get my property." Despite the harassment, Owen's wife and children remained safe and he was able to maintain at least some business revenue during the war years. "My income has been more than my expenses and my family are healthy. For these blessings I am thankful."[11]

Owen believed that the situation would improve in late 1862 when Union general Odon Guitar, a lawyer from Columbia, Missouri, arrived to take command of the troops stationed in and around St. Joseph. Guitar's intent was to rein in the lawless Union troops that had been preying on the city's Southern sympathizers. Guitar wanted to prosecute offenders and asked the provost marshal, Union commanders, and local citizenry to turn in Union soldiers who were causing trouble. Owen wrote that "thieves in the military service were arrested and brought to trial, and the perpetrators of outrages on the citizens were brought to justice." Taking Guitar at his word, Owen "dared to uphold openly [the Union's] policy [of turning in violent soldiers] and this gave offence to those who were robbing and murdering in the name of the Union and Liberty."[12]

For his bold actions, Owen became a target of rank-and-file Union soldiers, who set out to find and arrest him. "They picked a Sunday evening to elude their superior officers," Owen reported. "A Sergeant and eight men came to my house." When they discovered that he was not home, the men persuaded Mary, who was twelve or thirteen years old at the time, to lead them to a church where her father was found and apprehended. James Owen was detained overnight. Although no charges were filed against him, officials would only release Owen after he agreed to sign a loyalty oath.[13]

Even though James Owen took the oath, questions surrounding the sincerity of his loyalty shadowed him after the war. In this, Owen was certainly not alone. Postbellum Missouri proved to be an unfriendly place for thousands of Southern loyalists. At the war's end, Missouri citizens elected delegates to a new constitutional convention. While the convention was ostensibly called to formalize the abolition of slavery, the convention's vice president, the St. Louis lawyer and "Radical Republican" Charles Drake, persuaded the delegates that the 1820 constitution should be rewritten in order to help Missouri move forward from its slaveholding past. The so-called Drake Constitution, which was adopted April 8, 1865, famously included a provision called the "iron-clad oath." In order for Missouri men to vote, hold public office, teach school, or become ministers, the constitution stipulated that they had to sign an oath that they had never actively helped to advance the Southern cause during the war, that they had never supported the cause, and that they had never even spoken in favor of it. Naturally, the iron-clad oath prevented large numbers of men from participating in public life because of their disloyalty to the Union during the war years.[14]

Perhaps because many members of St. Joseph's business community had supported the South, the city was slow to recover from the virtual lockdown that had choked its citizens and businesses for most of the war. "This place has probably done an immense amount of business, in days gone by," wrote a Kansas City journalist who visited just months after fighting had ceased. "Those days will never return for St. Joseph. She is dead, dead; past resurrection."[15] So much of the pride and vitality that had buoyed the city's citizens before the war had evaporated by its end. The Pony Express, which had brought so much national attention to the city, had operated for just eighteen months and the Patee House Hotel was closed and shuttered by 1865. Even the city's crown jewel, the Hannibal and St. Joseph Railroad, had lost much of its luster because it had been heavily vandalized and was considered dangerous during the war. Hopes that the line would become part of the transcontinental railroad were crushed when it was announced the rails would run north through Omaha. Another trans-Missouri line would run from St. Louis to Kansas City, which by 1870 would surpass St. Joseph in population.

The war took a toll on the Owen family as well. Historian Sheridan Logan wrote that at the war's end, forty-three-year-old James Owen "retired" from business and turned his attention "to the management of his private affairs." Given the extent of the disenfranchisement of Southern loyalists—especially men—in the years immediately following the war, one wonders whether James Owen lost much of his business because of his outspoken advocacy of his political beliefs. Though Owen was still listed as a lawyer in the 1870 U.S. Census, the value of his properties had shrunken

James Alfred Owen, c. 1880. A successful businessman and lawyer, James Owen arrived in St. Joseph, Missouri, in 1847, just four years after the town was founded. While his marriage to Agnes Cargill allowed him to enter business with his wealthy father-in-law James Cargill, financial affairs and property disputes often led him to quarrel with members of the Cargill family. Owen's business interests also suffered because of his ardent support of the Southern cause during the Civil War. (Courtesy of the Missouri State Archives)

to $15,000, far below the $50,000 worth of property he had claimed at the beginning of the war.

We do not know exactly how the trauma of the war affected others in the Owen family. Given the treatment their father had received at the hands of Union men, many of whom had been their neighbors, members of the family may have felt that their community had betrayed them. Many Missouri families came out of those turbulent years with a deep distrust of the outside world. To compensate, it was not uncommon for Southern families to turn inward for support.

Scholars such as LeeAnn Whites have written about the changes in domestic life that were brought about by the Civil War, especially in Southern families. According to Whites, the violence of the war not only caused male Southern sympathizers like James Owen to lose economic power and prestige in their communities, it also caused them to lose authority they had held in their own homes. James Owen's imprisonment, the loss of his business, and reduction of his assets meant that it was more difficult for him to provide for his family. Whites argues that prior to the war, women had depended on the men in their families to "protect and defend" them by using their power outside the home to acquire wealth and status. With the defeat of the South and the disenchantment of Southern men, many like James Owen were forced to rely more heavily on the women in their lives to manage their households and help uphold the position of the family in the community. Southern women provided critical emotional support for men by urging them "to take solace in their own family circle, a family circle that should be more valued for that which had been lost." As a result, the dynamics of Southern families after the war became less stratified along gender lines.[16]

Fortunately for James Owen, his wife proved extremely capable in keeping the household intact. Agnes Cargill Owen, who celebrated her thirty-first birthday just a few months after the war began, took on the job of educating her children, who in 1861 ranged in age from eleven to two years old, at home after the schools that their two oldest daughters had attended, Mrs. Barker's and Miss Sarah Bell's private schools, were forced to close.[17] Jean Fahey Eberle has written that in teaching her daughters, Agnes Owen, who was well-educated and had some experience as a teacher, encouraged them to value education and to use the knowledge they gained to become self-reliant. Eberle asserts that Owen did not want her daughters to have to rely on men for their livelihoods, pushing them to feel confident in their ability to make their own way in the world.[18]

In the years after the Civil War, Agnes Owen also became responsible for much of the Owen family's long-term financial stability. It was she, after all, who was an heir to one-quarter of her mother's sizeable estate. Despite the looting of Burr Oak and the burning of Eagle Mill, Agnes Crookes Cargill's estate was valued at $75,000— or about $1.25 million in today's dollars—in the 1870 census. As such, Agnes Owen's expected share of the inheritance was worth more than her husband's war-ravaged portfolio of assets.[19]

It is worth noting that, while Mary Alicia Owen would one day write many stories and articles that, in one way or another, dealt with the history of St. Joseph and the state of Missouri, she would write nothing noteworthy about one of the most significant historical events of her lifetime, the Civil War. This seems to be a curious omission considering that she was eleven years old when the war began and would certainly have been aware of the conflict and the ways in which it directly touched her family. From the tone of his writings, it is obvious that James Owen held strong opinions about the war and undoubtedly would have aired those opinions in Mary's presence. The war interrupted her schooling and restricted her ability to leave the house and to move around town. The war even entered the Owen home in the form of Union soldiers intent on arresting Mary's father. The conflict, and the way it turned neighbors against one another, surely had a lasting effect on her life. Whether the war led her to remain more devoted to her family than she might otherwise have been, or whether it gave her the confidence to remain in St. Joseph and to seek out a career on her own, we may never know.

Though rampant violence and martial law had forced Mary to spend much of her adolescence confined to the safety of the Owen and Cargill family homes, she developed a strong outgoing personality. She was intellectually quick, immensely curious, and endowed with a self-effacing sense of humor that some have attributed to her self-consciousness about her physical appearance.[20] Freed from wartime restrictions and nearing the age when she would be introduced into society as a young woman, Owen, who was fifteen years old when the war ended, was eager to experience the outside world in ways that would one day raise the eyebrows of more than a few St. Joseph matrons.

Soon after the war ended, Mary resumed her education by attending Patee Female College, which opened in 1865 in the same four-story building that once housed the Patee House Hotel and the headquarters of the Pony Express. When the college closed in 1868, she made the bold decision to attend Vassar College in Poughkeepsie, New York. It is difficult to understand why a young Episcopalian with strong Southern roots would choose to travel more than twelve hundred miles to attend a nondenominational school in the postbellum North. While we may never know the precise reason Mary attended Vassar, one important factor in her decision may have been Sarah Josepha Hale.

A tireless crusader, Hale is perhaps best remembered as the author of the nursery rhyme "Mary had a Little Lamb" and as the person most responsible for making the celebration of Thanksgiving a national holiday. From 1837 until 1877, Hale was the editor of *Godey's Lady's Book*, a monthly magazine that reached more than 150,000 homes in 1860, making it one of the most popular periodicals in the United States at that time. *Godey's* was known for its wonderfully detailed fashion illustrations and for publishing original fiction and poetry by such noted authors as Edgar Allan Poe. Hale, who was also a published author, was committed to featuring the writing of women in the pages of *Godey's* and published some issues of the magazine that were devoted exclusively to fiction and poetry written by women. Mary Owen would herself publish at least one story in the magazine in the mid-1880s.[21]

Godey's was also known for its column the "Editor's Table," in which Hale advocated a number of causes. Among the topics that reached readers through Hale's editorials were gender roles, education, and medicine. In 1860, Sarah Hale turned her editorial gaze toward Matthew Vassar and the new women's college he was funding in New York. A wealthy brewer who lacked a formal education, Vassar sought to "build and endow a college for young women which shall be to them what Harvard and Yale are to young men." Unlike most three-year female seminaries of the day, which primarily focused on preparing women for careers in teaching, Vassar offered young women a broad liberal arts education and was among the first women's colleges in the United States to offer bachelor's degrees.[22]

After learning of Matthew Vassar's plans, Hale wrote him a letter offering her support for the project: "I shall be rejoiced to aid in your good plan, by making the readers of the *Lady's Book* your earnest friends, as they cannot help but honor a gentleman who is thus earnest to promote the true cultivation of femin[ine] talents. We want true women, trained in the full use of their *powers* of mind, heart, soul, and taught to devote all their talents as women."[23]

Vassar enthusiastically accepted Hale's offer, and the two began a correspondence that lasted until Vassar's death in 1868. Between 1860 and 1865, when the college opened its doors to students for the first time, Hale served as both an advocate for the school and an informal advisor to its benefactor. Because she had direct access to Matthew Vassar during those important years in the school's formation, Hale was able to exert a certain amount of influence in its final structure. She succeeded in persuading him to remove the word "female" from the college's proposed name, Vassar Female College. "Female!" she wrote in a letter to Matthew Vassar in March 1865. "What female do you mean? Not a female donkey? . . . why degrade the feminine sex to the level of animals?"[24] Sarah Hale also led the campaign to allow women to join the Vassar faculty by pointing out the inherent contradiction of a school for women that refused to employ women. When the college opened in September 1865, two of its eight professors were women. Hale advocated less successfully for the inclusion of domestic education courses in the curriculum. She believed that while women should be able to participate in the world outside the home, they should be competent in performing household tasks that would prepare them to assume a leadership role inside the home.[25]

Sarah Hale's most important contribution to Vassar College, however, may have been the many editorials she wrote about it in the pages of Godey's, beginning in October 1860. Better than any advertising the new college could have hoped for, Hale's editorials brought the school and its ideals to the attention of hundreds of thousands of people across the nation. Hale's attention was especially fortuitous for the new school because the population demographic that subscribed to Godey's was well matched with the segment of the population that would attend Vassar College. Both attracted affluent or upper-middle-class women who were interested in art, fashion, and domestic skills while being equally interested in advancing the opportunities open to women to work and flourish outside the home. Since Mary Alicia Owen came from a family that fit this description, and because it is not difficult to imagine that her family possessed the means and the literary interest to subscribe to Godey's, it is not so surprising that she became interested in attending Vassar College. Agnes Owen would have seen the college as the perfect place to reinforce in Mary the lessons of self-reliance and poise that she had taught her at home.

When Mary arrived in Poughkeepsie in the fall of 1868, Vassar College was beginning its fourth academic year. Mary's dormitory room and most of her classrooms were in a large, sprawling four-story main building, which also housed a dining room, library, and a chapel. Beyond the main building were an observatory and a gymnasium. Students studied such topics as elocution, studio art, logic, ornithology, and mineralogy and made occasional trips ninety miles down the Hudson River into New York City to attend concerts, art exhibits, and other cultural events. Vassar had dispensed with the tradition of forcing students to learn by rote memorization. Instead, classes were taught through "oral instruction," a style of classroom lecture and conversation that resembles the way classes are often taught today.[26] Ellen Swallow, one of Owen's Vassar schoolmates, likened the school to a "rose of sunlight breaking through the gray of women's intellectual life."[27] A young woman who attended Vassar the year after Owen was there wrote home to exclaim, "Why have they not started some such college as this long ago, where women could learn to be independent . . . it is the well equipped woman who gets the job and is able to hold it."[28]

Because Owen remained quiet about her year at Vassar, we do not know whether she echoed the sentiments expressed by her schoolmates. Jean Eberle has suggested that Owen's experience at Vassar was not a pleasant one because her Southern heritage made her an outsider in the postwar North. While Owen was certainly not the only Southern woman to attend Vassar, she was definitely in the minority. Historian Joan Marie Johnson writes that between 1865 and 1925, Southern women made up between 3 and 10 percent of the student population. She found that Southern women who attended schools in the North often found themselves mocked for their accents and expressions and for their support of the lost cause of the Confederacy. In some cases, Johnson writes, this led women to embrace their Southern identity even more wholeheartedly. While there would be Southern social clubs at Vassar in the late nineteenth century, there is no mention of them having existed while Owen attended.[29] Her attempts to fit in at Vassar may have been further complicated by the fact that, in addition to being a Southerner, she was a Westerner who had grown up on the very edge of the American frontier. In 1868, the West was still perceived by many in the East as an untamed land of savage Indians and wild animals. It would have been easy for students at Vassar to assume that Owen, as a daughter of the frontier, was rustic in her manners and dull in her wits. Eberle contends that Owen's unhappiness at Vassar prompted her to leave the school after just one year. While this may have been the case, it is also possible that Owen, who was nineteen years old at the end of her year at Vassar, felt that she was old enough to conclude her formal education and embark on a career.

In either case, Owen's experiences at Vassar, like her experiences during the war, seem to have left their mark on her. In later life, Mary Alicia Owen came to embody many of the characteristics Sarah Josepha Hale and Matthew Vassar hoped to develop in Vassar College students. Strong-willed, self-confident, and intellectually inquisitive, Owen, whose family's wealth had made her financially secure, would never marry and allow herself to become reliant on a husband for her livelihood. Always determined to do things her own way, she possessed both the persistence to work toward the goals she set for herself and the courage to enter and succeed in the male-dominated fields of literature and folklore.

Three

A Literary Life, 1870–1890

By the time she returned to St. Joseph in 1869, Mary Alicia Owen seems to have set her sights on a career as a writer. She was fortunate in that her family's circumstances afforded her the leisure to make life choices based on her interests rather than on the pursuit of financial stability. Women of her social standing had to be careful in pursuing a career because they faced the real prospect of losing their status if it became known that they worked outside the home. Historian Janice Brandon-Falcone has observed that this was especially difficult for women of Owen's social class who, for one reason or another, were unable to support themselves. Because wage labor was judged to be beneath women of status, those who were forced to work out of necessity found few options open to them. Brandon-Falcone notes that the St. Joseph culture maven Constance Runcie faced this dilemma after her husband James, a minister in the Christ Episcopal Church, died in the late 1880s. For a woman of Runcie's standing, who could not make ends meet without her husband's income, only occupations that could be performed inside her home were acceptable. While some women augmented their incomes by teaching students or by giving music lessons, Runcie survived by presenting concerts and lectures inside her large house.

For Owen, who appears to have decided early in life to forgo marriage and the prospect of dependence on a man, a literary career was ideal. It allowed her to engage her intellect and imagination even as she remained at home on Ninth Street with her parents and siblings. In her early career as a writer, Owen most often submitted her stories to publishers under the pseudonym Julia Scott. This leads us to wonder if Owen, or members of her family, worried that even writing might be considered to be an unseemly occupation for a woman of standing.[1]

Before leaving for Vassar, Owen had begun to give readings at meetings of one of the young women's social clubs to which she belonged. According to Brandon-Falcone, nineteenth-century study and literary clubs provided women with an outlet for their creativity and intellectual interests. The clubs created "a safe, nonpublic place where they could present to one another essays, poetry and stories they had written."[2] While the gregarious Owen likely enjoyed the opportunity to speak in front of others, the readings also allowed her to commit some of her own story ideas to paper. "It was natural, I think, that [Mary] began to write when she returned from Vassar," Juliette Owen told a newspaper reporter in 1941. "She started by contributing a column on old settlers to a weekly newspaper, *The Saturday Democrat*, I believe it was called, and by composing bits of verse . . . Soon, she was trying her hand at letters of travel, book reviews and short stories." George E. King, an Indiana native who had practiced law and taught school in Missouri, published the *St. Joseph Saturday Democrat* for only four years, from about 1879 to 1883. Because the paper was short-lived and copies are difficult to find, scholars have yet to identify the writings Owen produced for it.[3]

In time, Mary recognized that new opportunities in the expanding world of publishing allowed her to write for a broader regional and even national audience. After the Civil War, the popular press exploded with a new array of periodicals, many of which were looking for writers to contribute short stories. Owen discovered that she had a knack for producing two kinds of stories for which magazine publishers had a need. She was able to write stories with romantic plots that were aimed specifically at the growing audience of women readers. Owen also found that she was adept at drawing upon her experiences as a Missourian to write what were known at the time as local-color stories. Beginning in 1870, Owen, usually writing under the name Julia Scott, published poems and short fiction in magazines such as *The Century, Ballou's Monthly Magazine, Prairie Farmer,* and *Overland Magazine.*

While Owen's biographers have often alluded to her early poems and stories, the works themselves have been overlooked. Perhaps because a complete bibliography of Mary Alicia Owen's published stories and poems has never been compiled, none of the scholars who have written about her in the past have given any of these works more than a passing mention. This is unfortunate because a sample of her stories reveals much about Owen's development and maturation as a writer. They show us that she not only possessed a quick wit, a flair for sentiment, and a keen eye for local flavor, but that she addressed topics and themes that would emerge in her later academic career as a folklorist. Because her early verse and fiction helped to lay the groundwork for those later works, it is important to take a look at a few of the stories Mary Alicia Owen published between 1870 and 1890.

Romance is at the heart of each of the works Owen is known to have published in the popular press. As Henry Nash Smith has pointed out, romantic fiction helped to sooth the anxiety that seemed to permeate the upwardly mobile middle class of the Victorian era. Smith writes that readers needed to be reassured that, even in a rapidly changing world, the "realm of the Ideal was predictable" even when it was achieved in mysterious ways. Thus, readers of the era found comfort in romantic story plots that, while often contrived, led to conventional outcomes.[4] In the mid-nineteenth century, such fiction drove the sale of magazines, especially those geared toward women, and Owen proved to be quite able at developing clever variations on the typical boy-meets-girl formula. She knew how to write both light romance and overwrought melodrama and, most importantly, she knew how to produce endings that conformed to the expectations of her audience.

In "Jack Looking for a Jill," a story that appeared in *Peterson's Magazine* in September 1884, Captain Jack Heath, a man of independent means from New York City's "fashionable world," expresses his belief that a country girl—a girl reared in the hills who possesses "good health, high principles, plenty of affection, and noble ideas"—would make the ideal bride.[5] "I am sick of those overdressed girls, who are fawning or pert, according to the game they're after," he loudly complains while attending a society ball in fashionable Cape May, New Jersey. For this reason, Jack makes a show of turning down an opportunity to be introduced to Miss Winter, a highly sought-after heiress with "connections to one of the best families in Philadelphia." "If I ever find a wife, it will not be in a ball-room," Miss Winter overhears Jack say to a friend.

Some days later, Jack chances to meet the same Miss Winter while he is traveling in the Allegheny Mountains. While Jack does not recognize the young woman, whose real name is Gussie Harmon, she remembers him. Recalling his rebuff at the ball, she makes no mention of the event to Jack and he is none the wiser. Over the course of a few weeks, the couple has the opportunity to spend time together at the home Gussie shares with her stepfather. Jack falls in love with Gussie and, as he prepares to leave, asks for her hand in marriage. She refuses and Jack returns to New York brokenhearted.

Sometime later, a friend persuades Jack, who is still despondent over his failure to win Gussie's love, to meet Miss Winter at a social function in New York. Only then does Jack realize that Miss Winter and Gussie Harmon are one and the same. She explained to the surprised captain that while she lived with her stepfather, Doctor Harmon, she sometimes stayed with her uncle, Mr. Winter, while attending school in the city. During the time that she had spent with Jack in the mountains, Gussie had been afraid to tell him that she was the same woman he had shunned at the ball in Cape May, yet she felt that she could not accept his marriage proposal until the matter was cleared up. Jack accepts both Gussie's explanation and her identity as a society woman, and the couple is married soon after.

In several of Owen's short stories, misunderstandings related to identity, social class, and wealth serve as obstacles in romantic courtship. Jack Heath's misperceptions of young society women kept him from seeing Gussie Harmon/Miss Winter for who she really was. Similarly, young Toinette, the protagonist in a story called "The Exile's Daughter," published in *Godey's Lady's Book* in 1885, turns down a marriage proposal from Colonel Dick Graham because she wrongly suspects that he is trying to embezzle her family's fortune.[6] Unknown to Toinette, Graham, who had served as her legal guardian until she turned eighteen, is being pursued by Mrs. Etynge, a widow who is one of Toinette's confidants and something of a gold-digger. Because Mrs. Etynge suspects that Graham is in love with his former ward, she convinces Toinette that the colonel had profited personally through his mismanagement of her trust fund.

As Toinette prepares to leave Graham's home to live with her father, the colonel confesses his love for her and asks her to marry him. Angry because she believes he has been stealing from her, Toinette refuses the proposal. Only months later, when she hears that the colonel is to marry Mrs. Etynge, does Toinette realize that she has been deceived, not by the colonel but by her friend the widow. When word comes that the colonel is gravely ill, Toinette rushes to his side and, learning that he will not marry Mrs. Etynge after all, eagerly agrees to become his wife.

"The New Tenor," a melodrama that appeared in 1890 in *Frank Leslie's Popular Monthly*, also deals with a deception.[7] When St. Cecilia's Church advertises that they need a tenor to sing in the choir, dark handsome Victor Heath is the only singer to respond. While everyone in the choir is taken with Victor and his rich voice, his singing has a special effect on Alice, the young organist whom Owen describes as the "fairest flower in [the congregation's] garden of girls." Alice becomes the singer's regular accompanist, and as winter turns to spring, the couple spends hours together in rehearsal. Just as their relationship begins to blossom, a "fierce, gypsy-looking creature," appears, claiming that she is Victor Heath's wife. Victor looks stricken as the woman drags him away and Alice is heartbroken and angry at having allowed herself to be deceived by a married man.

Later, Victor returns to ask Alice's forgiveness. While admitting that he was married, he explained the circumstances that led to the unhappy union. He had been orphaned at seventeen and was alone in New York. While still very young, he had joined a second-rate opera company and allowed himself to fall under the influence of the company's much older prima donna. Soon after they married, Mrs. Heath abandoned her young husband yet refused to allow him to divorce her. Several times the young man had tried to leave his wife and find happiness elsewhere, but he could never escape. Having told his story, he leaves Alice in tears as a spring rain begins to fall. Just outside Alice's yard, however, Victor's jealous wife pounces on him and kills him with a dagger. The story closes with the unnamed narrator noting, "Some lives are to humanity a song, and some a sermon, and a blessed few 'purified by fire,' a benediction."

Perhaps it is not surprising that these tales of Gilded Age romance involve characters that live—or aspire to live—on the upper rungs of the economic ladder. Owen was herself a member of an affluent family and was certainly conscious of class distinction. Similarly, America as a whole seemed to be preoccupied with wealth and class during the 1870s, 1880s, and 1890s. Rapid industrial growth in the decades following the Civil War had given rise to an expanding class of extremely wealthy captains of finance and industry. Men with names like Vanderbilt, Morgan, Rockefeller, and Carnegie captured the public imagination by setting the standard for extravagant mansions and opulent lifestyles. Henry Nash Smith reminds us that because such men were often self-made millionaires, they saw themselves as "representatives of the common people." Nonetheless, they also saw themselves as role models for proper American social taste and morality. Because writers like Owen were often members of the upper or middle class, they too felt it was their responsibility to uphold morality by placing socially acceptable restraints on their characters. For this reason, Owen's protagonists often faced morally ambiguous situations but always negotiated them with decorum. Those, like the married tenor Victor Heath, whose behavior did not live up to Victorian norms, paid a tragic price. Such was the code of honor that Owen's readers expected.[8]

Mary Alicia Owen did not set all of her romances in the world of the well-heeled. She placed some of her stories in the locale she knew and understood better than any other, western Missouri. Owen's career as a writer coincided with a push from various literary circles to create fiction that was uniquely American in character. While the reading public never seemed to tire of stories depicting romance among the wealthy, such stories were not unique to the United States. Nineteenth-century America did, however, have something to which Europe could not lay claim, a vast landscape that included dense forests, mighty rivers, and of course, the Wild West. In the decades after the Civil War, the rugged landscape captured the American imagination as a place that possessed its own sublime romance. It was untamed, picturesque, and filled with dangerous natives and outlaws. The United States also possessed a wide array of distinct population groups with strong regional characteristics. The reading public's interest in stories that included America's unique people and landscape gave rise to a popular genre known as "local color" stories. According to literary historian Bernd C. Peyer, local-color stories were "characterized by a focus on regional settings and representations of customs, costumes, and dialects of the people living there."[9] With its picturesque landscape and diverse population of African Americans, American Indians, and immigrants from various European countries, western Missouri was an ideal location for local-color source material. Using experiences she may have gained while writing articles about St. Joseph's old settlers and regional history for a local newspaper, Owen was able to create characters and situations that reflected the characteristics and diversity of the region.

Owen's earliest known published work was a poem called "The Bride's Farewell," which appeared under her own name in *Prairie Farmer* in 1870, just a year after she left Vassar. The poem broadly fits the local-color genre in that it portrays a new farm bride as she bids farewell to her childhood home and her family as she prepares to leave them for a new life with her husband.

> This home I have loved, oh, fondly,
> And there dear friends I know are true.
> But I now leave them all dear husband,
> For the love I have for you.[10]

Clearly, the farm bride's thoughts, as she prepares to wed, are focused on the home that she will lose in her new role as wife. The compromise of marriage is a topic that Owen visits in more than one of her local-color stories. In "Patty's Literary Experiences," which appeared in 1884, a young small-town Missouri woman also makes compromises in the name of marriage. Plain-looking Patty Brown endeavors to satisfy her poetic aspirations by covering society events for Colonel McFad's local newspaper, the *Chanticleer*. However, "Higginsville's favorite poetess" is soon inundated by petty complaints from several class-conscious women who do not care for the way she has portrayed them in print. One local matron is irate because she expected Patty to embellish a description of her muslin gown by reporting that it was made of "surah silk." Another woman takes offense when Patty describes her party dress as being "sprigged" rather than "brocaded." Dissatisfied with society news, Patty tries a short and equally unsatisfactory assignment at the paper's obituary desk. Finally, she confronts the colonel with the intention of resigning from the paper in frustration. However, it becomes clear that McFad hired Patty not because of her talent but because he was smitten with her. He responds to her resignation by telling her that all he has left to offer her is "me, my family, my housekeeping." Sensing that the offer allows her a chance at the financial security that her poetic endeavors are unlikely to win her, Patty agrees to become the wife of the much older—and very wealthy—colonel.[11]

The social aspirations, class consciousness, and bourgeois preoccupations of the small-town residents of western Missouri are other themes that appear in more than one example of Owen's early fiction. While Patty Brown ascends a step on the social ladder in exchange for her ambitions as a poet, the protagonist of "Miss Dolly's Ideals" (1887) is not so fortunate. Dolly Meacham, the daughter of a widow and a "lovely little simpleton," desires nothing more than to have a poetic name and live a regal life. "I'd like to be called Dorthea or Theodora and marry a lord, dressed in crimson plush," Dolly confides to her maid, the poetically named Althea. Standing in the way of Dolly's dream, however, is Althea's brother and Dolly's suitor, Tom Potts. "Poor Tom!" Dolly laments, "He is not poetical enough to dream about." Though Dolly rebuffs Tom, she becomes jealous when he attracts the attention of Miss Sweetser, a young woman from a nearby town whom Dolly disdains as an "underbred creature" who is unworthy of his affection. Suddenly faced with competition for Tom's attention, Dolly realizes that "she is in love with Tom, fat, untitled, plebian-named Tom." She agrees to be his wife and accepts the fact that she "will have a common place house, a common place husband, and be called Dolly Potts for the rest of [her] days."[12]

The compromises endured by Patty Brown, Dolly Meacham, and the unnamed narrator of "The Bride's Farewell" were not unique in fiction written in an era that placed a strong emphasis on conformity and obedience to authority. In the late nineteenth century, men most often possessed absolute power in domestic situations. According to Henry Nash Smith, the father figure in Victorian fiction often represents a kind of "secular divinity" that had absolute control over social situations. If a female character was to rise in social status, says Smith, she had to acquiesce to that authority. Ironically, while these stories reflected a broad social norm for the era, they did not reflect Owen's own circumstances. Though her father managed to remain active in business and society after the Civil War, Mary lived in a home that was notable for the strength of its women.[13]

It is worth noting that while the characters Owen creates in her Missouri stories sometimes marry others from outside their economic status, they do not tend to marry people from outside their community. Outsiders, like the overly flirtatious Miss Sweetser, are not generally welcomed into Owen's close-knit fictional communities. Such is the case in the story "Phoebus or Cupid," which appeared in 1886. Professor Timotheus N. Jones, an outsider who is also the assistant state entomologist, becomes infatuated with Rosa Allen, the "most beautiful blonde lady he had ever beheld," while traveling on a study expedition in the country. As a man of science, Jones is unsure how to react to his feelings and how to respond to the rapt attention with which Miss Allen favors him. Over time, he convinces himself that she is in love with him and that, despite the fact that it would interrupt his research and his unfinished book, he must marry her.

On the evening that he plans to propose to Miss Allen, Jones discovers that she is actually in love with Walter Stacey, a local man who has been away during the professor's visit. While she had enjoyed the diversion of his long monologues about insects and had viewed him as a pleasant curiosity, she had apparently never considered Timotheus as a potential husband. The professor is surprised to find that he is only mildly disappointed by this revelation, and he happily returns to his own world, where he is quickly absorbed in his work. When he learns that Walter Stacey and Rosa Allen have married, he sends the newlyweds a valuable collection of grasshoppers as a wedding present.[14]

In 1889, Owen published a story that focused more specifically on the history, customs, and cultural diversity of her hometown. "The Taming of Tarias," which appeared under Owen's own name, tells the story of Tarias Beauvais, a twenty-year-old Métis woman. Residents of the Blacksnake Hills call Tarias "the Queen" because her father was a French trapper and her mother was the "descendant of the rightful lords of the soil, the Chiefs of the Sacs and Foxes." Tarias has a reputation for being strong willed or, as one local bluntly observes, "She's French quick an' Injun stubborn." While many men had tried to woo her, conventional wisdom in the community holds that no man is her match. "It don't pay to rile her," another local advises. To this last remark, blond, handsome Dave Potts, a recent transplant from Kentucky, offers the opinion that "all she needs is tamin'." To which he adds, "She ain't mean and she ain't cruel, she's jist wild."

Dave sets out to introduce himself to the Queen. Through a series of coincidences, he accompanies Tarias and her brother to a country dance one evening. The crowd takes note of the fact that while Tarias "ain't never danced 'ith *our* boys," she remains on the floor with Dave throughout the evening. As one of Tarias's former suitors jealously speculates that the newcomer Dave had likely "be'n run outen his own State fur hoss-stealin'" and was not worthy of the Queen's attention, a drunken magistrate, prompted by some equally inebriated comrades, pronounces the two "husband and wife" on the dance floor.

"With her scepter broken in her hand by the cruel bludgeon of a practical joker," the Queen is crushed. Terrified that marriage will enslave her, she resists her family's attempts to talk her into acknowledging her new role as Dave's wife. As Dave too desperately tries to convince her of his love, Tarias literally strikes out at him, cutting him in the cheek with a knife. The six-month-long standoff that follows is broken only when Tarias discovers that a gang of men is on its way to Dave's cabin to settle a dispute they had with him in the past. Intent on warning Dave of the danger, the Queen makes a dramatic dash through the woods on a dark January evening. With wolves nipping at her heels, she manages to reach his cabin ahead of the gang of men and the wolves. After reaching the cabin, Tarias is relieved to find that Dave is safe. He, in turn, is touched at her willingness to risk her life to warn him. In the light of this epiphany, the couple reconciles. Tarias, it appears, has been tamed.[15]

"The Taming of Tarias" was a breakthrough for Owen. Of all her local-color stories, it offers the most complete picture of the St. Joseph of her youth. The story focuses on the various ethnic groups and social classes that populated the settlement in the years before the Civil War. In "The Taming of Tarias," Owen portrays the French traders, like Antoine Beauvais, Tarias's father, and "Uncle" Joe Robidoux, who, as the region's earliest nonnative inhabitants, are both the cultural and financial foundation of the community. She portrays the merchants, businessmen, and speculators, like her father and maternal grandfather, who helped turn the trading post into a small thriving city. Alongside these local magnates, Owen contrasts backwoods society, represented by Kentucky-born Dave and the Métis Tarias.

Yet while the St. Joseph of Owen's story is multicultural and multiethnic, it is not, for the most part, a melting pot. People are largely segregated by race and by their place in the social and economic strata. Tarias in particular is defined by her racial background. Readers learn that her Sac and Fox heritage exhibits itself in her stubbornness, her experience in the ways of the wild, a contentious spirit, and an air of superiority. Owen also shows her readers that even though Tarias is a native of the Blacksnake Hills and has deep roots in the community, white settlers consider her to be an outsider because of her Sac and Fox ancestry. By allowing Dave—an outsider by virtue of the fact that he came from rural Kentucky—to successfully "tame" Tarias, Owen reinforces the social order of her time, which mandated that it was best for "untamed" backwoods people to stick to their own and to be excluded from the more established and "civilized" community.

"The Taming of Tarias" is the first story in which Owen's characters speak in vernacular dialect. In most fiction of that era, dialect was reserved for those characters who lived on the lower rungs of the social ladder, the type of characters Henry Nash Smith has called "nongenteel." Cultural historian Alan Trachtenberg has pointed out that the use of dialect had first emerged in local-color stories before the Civil War, but its use spread widely after the war. In most cases, dialect was used as a way of signifying that certain characters were culturally inferior to the story's writer and to its readers. By employing dialect in a story, authors were acknowledging the social perspective of the mostly middle- and upper-class whites who wrote, published, and consumed fiction in postbellum America. Because they were bound to uphold proper Victorian standards of taste and morality, writers were free to include "low" characters in their fiction, as long as they made it clear that they, the writers, possessed moral propriety that was distinct and above that of their characters'. By using dialect, writers could make that distinction clear without stating it overtly.[16]

It could be argued that Mary Alicia Owen used dialect in "The Taming of Tarias" as a way of attempting to give the story a greater sense of authenticity. Four years earlier, Mark Twain had succeeded in doing just that by having Huckleberry Finn narrate the story of his adventures in the dialect of an uneducated Missourian. Trachtenberg writes that the device worked for Twain in part because the narrator's use of dialect made it difficult for readers to discern where the character's voice ended and the author's voice began. Twain made no distinction between his taste and morals and those of his protagonist. In "Tarias," however, Owen's use of dialect can be seen as a signifier of class rather than as an element of realism, in part because her position as upholder of proper standards of morality and taste are never in doubt.

The way in which Owen depicts her characters in the "Taming of Tarias" leads us to wonder if she did not feel some anxiety over the rapid changes she had seen St. Joseph undergo during her lifetime. By 1889, when the story was published, St. Joseph was a far different place than it had been when she was a child. The economic stagnation that had so worried local boosters at the end of the Civil War had long since vanished and the city's economy and population had mushroomed. Transplanted settlers from the eastern United States and immigrants from Europe helped St. Joseph grow from less than 20,000 people in 1870 to more than 52,000 in 1890—an increase of more than 150 percent.

In those two decades, St. Joseph had built an opera house, a new city hall, and a new county courthouse. In 1886, the *Chicago Tribune* reported that the city was the home of thirteen miles of paved streets, 170 factories, and the largest stockyard west of Chicago. Boosted by wholesale dry goods, banking, and livestock trading, the city claimed to be "without a commercial or financial rival in the State of Missouri," excepting St. Louis.[17] While these dramatic changes made St. Joseph an economically vibrant place in which to live, they threatened the entrenched hegemony of economically privileged families like the Owens and Cargills, who saw themselves as the foundation of the community.

Historian Robert H. Wiebe has written that prominent Victorian families sometimes worried about the rapid pace of social and economic change that took place during the Gilded Age. Many, he writes, feared that America was under attack "from foes of extraordinary raw strength," which included "huge devouring [corporate] monopolies, swarms of sexually potent immigrants, and the like." He continues, "Mixing contempt with fear, [established citizens] pictured newcomers as dispirited breeders of poverty, crime, political corruption, and simultaneously as peculiarly powerful subversives." In this light, the sense of social hierarchy that characterized the world Owen created in "The Taming of Tarias" was very much in step with the broader attempt by Americans of her class and social position to preserve their privileged status in a rapidly changing world.[18]

While St. Joseph's growth had brought with it much that Owen may have found unsettling, it also served to further transform the city from the small settlement it had been in her youth. With every new paved street and glass-fronted retail establishment that was completed during the 1870s and 1880s, St. Joseph lost a piece of its picturesque frontier past. Joseph Robidoux, the city's beloved founder and a symbol of its pioneer days, had died at age eighty-five in 1868. Fourteen years later, the infamous outlaw Jesse James, a figure that was emblematic of the city's rugged days as the gateway to the Wild West, was shot to death in a house about a dozen blocks away from the Owen home. Log trading posts had long since been replaced with multistory banks, and cattle had replaced buffalo as the fuel that powered the city's economic engine.

Owen's "The Taming of Tarias," with its rugged characters and wilderness backdrop, expresses nostalgia for a time when St. Joseph was smaller and less refined and was considered to be the western-most outpost of civilization. Owen was certainly not alone in her longing for days gone by. By the time the story was published, a wave of post-frontier wistfulness had spread throughout the nation. By 1890, U.S. census figures indicated that the American frontier was, for all practical purposes, gone and all available land had been settled. In response to that declaration, historian Frederick Jackson Turner famously expressed his belief that the taming of the frontier had been the defining element of the American character. With the passing of this phase of its development, Turner warned, the nation would focus more on contemplating what it had lost in its rush to settle the continent.[19]

As St. Joseph grew and changed during the decades of the 1870s and 1880s, life in the Owen household changed as well. James Owen had briefly reentered the world of politics in 1876 when he ran for the office of lieutenant governor on the Greenback Party ticket. The Greenback Party distrusted large banks and corporate monopolies and ran on a platform that opposed the nation's return to a gold-bullion-based monetary system. Given that large banks and business monopolies were associated with Northern states, it is not surprising that Owen, who remained an unrepentant Southerner, was attracted to the party. While the Greenback Party ultimately achieved some success in the Midwest, winning a handful of congressional seats in Iowa, Illinois, and Missouri, Owen lost in his only bid for statewide office to a Democrat, Norman J. Colman.

In the decades after the Civil War, the dynamics of the Owen household changed as Mary's siblings had grown and begun their own lives. Two siblings had married in the 1880s. Florence Owen married William Bard Orr in 1881 and moved to Pittsburg, Pennsylvania. Hebert Owen married Harriet C. Kearney in 1882. Kearny was from a well-known family whose roots in the Missouri River valley ran back even farther than those of the Owen family. Her grandfather was Stephen Watts Kearney. As commander at Fort Leavenworth in the early 1830s, Kearney, then a colonel, had participated in some of the treaty negotiations that had removed the Ioway and Sac and Fox from the Blacksnake Hills. Before his marriage, Herbert had spent a year as a cadet at the West Point military academy. After an injury cut short his military career, he returned to St. Joseph where he worked as a newspaperman, a banker, and a real estate agent. After being admitted to the bar, he became president of a local abstract company.[20]

Like Mary, two other Owen girls did not marry. Luella and Juliette both continued to live in the family home after graduating from high school and, like their oldest sister, both pursued academic careers. Luella was salutatorian of her class when she graduated from St. Joseph Public High School in 1872. While little is known about her life before 1890, Luella did not attend college. Instead, she undertook the independent study of geology. Legend has it that while still a child, Luella became fascinated with the geological makeup of the St. Joseph's loess hills after seeing a road crew cut into a loess bank near her home. As Luella began to read various books on geology, she initiated correspondence with some of the scientists and authors she admired. Among these authors were George Frederick Wright, a minister and professor of literature at Oberlin College in Ohio. Though not trained in geology, Wright traveled widely and published books and articles on the topic. She also corresponded with James E. Todd, a professor at Tabor College in Hillsboro, Kansas, who also served as South Dakota state geologist. A third correspondent was University of Minnesota professor Newton Horace Winchell. At their suggestion, Luella Owen focused her early studies on the unique loess hills of the Missouri River valley.

Like her sister Luella, Juliette, the youngest of the Owen children, received most of her professional education at home. An accomplished artist, Juliette Owen also studied ornithology and botany. She was especially inspired by the work of the artist and ornithologist John James Audubon, who had visited the Blacksnake Hills in 1843. Like her sisters, Juliette would publish articles about the topics that interested her. She would also go on to provide illustrations for Mary's first book.

Juliette Amelia Owen, c. 1900. The youngest of the Owen children, Juliette lived her entire life in the family home at the corner of Ninth and Jules Streets in St. Joseph, dying in 1945 in the same room in which she had been born eighty-five years earlier. Juliette Owen was ornithologist and an artist who illustrated her sister Mary Alicia Owen's first book *Old Rabbit, the Voodoo, and Other Sorcerers*. (Courtesy of the Missouri State Archives)

Though the three Owen sisters remained in the home in which they grew up, caring for their aging parents, they did not live sheltered or reclusive lives. From all accounts, the Owen household was one in which intellectual pursuits and the discussion of ideas were given free rein. All three Owen daughters read voraciously and collected books and periodicals on a wide range of topics. They also kept busy with church activities, study groups, and social clubs, and they had the opportunity to travel regularly. Yet, as complete as their lives may have seemed, as the decade of the 1880s drew to a close, changes were coming that would propel all three sisters to the attention of scholars and admirers from outside their community. Mary in particular was soon to embark on a path that would lead to wide professional recognition and even a certain degree of fame. Perhaps it is fitting for a woman who was a voracious reader and a gifted writer that Mary Alicia Owen's journey to fame was to begin with the gift of a single book.

Four

"The White Voodoo," 1889–1891

To understand the cosmopolitan atmosphere that defined St. Joseph, Missouri, during the 1880s, consider the fact that the friend who lent Mary Alicia Owen the book that changed her life was the daughter of a well-known British astronomer. Olivia Proctor's father, Richard Anthony Proctor, lived in St. Joseph from 1884 to 1887. The elder Proctor was the author of more than two dozen books and had conducted an extensive study of the geographical features and rotational axis of the planet Mars. A widower, who according to various sources had either five or six children, Professor Proctor had moved to Missouri after marrying Sadie Crowley, the niece of former St. Joseph mayor and Civil War hero M. Jeff Thompson. Crowley's husband had died and left her with two children shortly before she met Proctor. According to Jean Fahey Eberle, Luella Owen studied astronomy with Professor Proctor, and members of the Owen and Proctor households regularly engaged in a lively exchange of books, articles, and ideas.[1]

In 1888, Olivia Proctor lent her friend Mary Owen a copy of *Algonquin Legends of New England* written by poet, humorist, and folklorist Charles Godfrey Leland. Leland was born in 1824 to Charles Leland and Charlotte Godfrey Leland in Philadelphia, Pennsylvania. Later in his life, Charles Godfrey Leland loved to tell people that his nurse had initiated him into the occult while he was still an infant. He elaborated on the incident in his *Memoirs*:

> I should mention that my first nurse in life was an old Dutch woman named Van der Poel. I had not been born many days be-

fore I and my cradle were missing. There was a prompt outcry and search, and both were soon found in the garret or loft of the house. There I lay sleeping, on my breast an open Bible, with, I believe, a key and knife, at my head lighted candles, money, and a plate of salt. Nurse Van der Poel explained that it was done to secure my rising in life by taking me up to the garret.[2]

After graduating from Princeton in 1845, Leland sailed for Europe to study in Germany and France. While living as a student in Paris in 1848, he participated in the February revolution that helped bring down the Orleans monarchy. Returning to study and practice law in Philadelphia, Leland soon became a journalist, working for newspapers and magazines in his hometown and in New York. In 1856, he married Eliza Bella "Isabel" Fisher. A staunch abolitionist, Leland served a brief stint in the Union army during the Civil War. After the war, he and his wife returned to Europe, where they spent much of the rest of their lives. In 1888, the year Owen first read *Algonquin Legends*, Charles Leland was probably best known as the author of *Hans Breitmenn Ballads*, a collection of comic poems written in a mixture of English and German.

Written in 1884, *Algonquin Legends of New England* was an anthology of more than seventy legends that Leland collected from tribes belonging to the Wabanaki Confederacy, the Passamaquoddies and Penobscots of Maine, and of the Mi'kmaqs of New Brunswick in 1882. As she read the book, Owen recognized striking similarities between the stories Leland had collected and those she had heard from Mymee Whitehead, Aunt Mary, and other African Americans she knew in St. Joseph. The stories, it turned out, owed at least as much to American Indian oral tradition as they did to African American influences. In the book, Leland included a footnote in which he asked for his readers' help in tracking down more Algonquin stories for publication.[3] In a move that would change her life forever, an excited Owen wrote the author. Her correspondence with Leland, who was living in Italy at the time, opened the door to a personal and professional relationship that lasted for fifteen years until Leland's death in 1903. More importantly, it launched the thirty-nine-year-old Owen on a new career as a folklorist and ethnologist.

While we do not know the contents of Mary Owen's first letter to Charles Leland, we do know that it included an example of at least one story that she had heard in Missouri. Leland responded

Charles Godfrey Leland, c. 1853. Charles Leland began his career as a journalist working for publications in New York and in his hometown of Philadelphia. The author of more than twenty books on American Indians, Gypsies, witches, folksongs, and fairies, Leland became Mary Alicia Owen's mentor after the two exchanged letters in 1889. (Courtesy of the Library of Congress)

enthusiastically to Owen on April 21, 1889, thanking her for the story and asking her to send material that he might be able to use in a "Great American Dictionary" of "queer words, phrases, rhymes, [and] charms" on which he was then working.[4]

While he was duly impressed with the depth of this amateur's knowledge of African American and American Indian folklore, Leland was astonished to learn that Owen had collected her stories in and around the western American city that had been her lifelong home. She "was not only born and brought up . . . among the most 'superstitious' race conceivable," Leland marveled years later, "but had from infancy an intense desire, aided by a marvelous memory, to collect and remember all that she learned. . . . In all my experience I never met but one person so perfectly at home in the subject [of Algonquin folklore], and that was a full-blood Passamaquoddy Indian . . . who had . . . collected all the folklore . . . of his tribe."[5]

Given the breadth of Owen's reading, it seems likely that she knew about the academic discipline of folklore before she began to correspond with Leland. But it also seems likely that she had never considered that her own stockpile of stories, songs, and rhymes could be of interest to members of the folklore community. Owen's correspondence with Leland appears to have quickly led her to reconsider her career as a writer, and within months of their initial contact, Leland began to mentor Owen in the process of collecting folklore. He advised her to write down as many stories as she could remember. "Never neglect to write down any story whatever, however feeble or uninteresting or petty or repeated it may seem. Some detail which may not strike you may be the missing link to a stupendous chain of discovery." He encouraged her to publish her findings and offered to introduce her to the editors of such publications as *Folk-Lore Journal.* Early in their correspondence, he also suggested that she write a book of folklore. "You can't make much money by it," he warned her, "but such a book gives a name now that folk-lore is all the fashion."[6]

Leland was fascinated by various kinds of witchcraft and considered himself to be a practitioner of magic. In his letters to Owen, he wrote extensively of his considerable experience in the occult and described for her the various charms he had collected. After learning that Owen had grown up around conjurers and that hoodoo was still practiced in Missouri, he strongly encouraged her to gather all she could on the topic.

Hoodoo has long gone by many different names. Because of its association with the religions of the Caribbean, many nineteenth-century whites like Mary Alicia Owen tended to refer to it incorrectly as *voodoo.* African Americans often referred to it as hoodoo, though historian Jeffrey E. Anderson writes that in Missouri, *noodoo* was the preferred term. Depending on where one lived in the United States, conjurer spells were called gris gris, mojo, rootwork, gombre-work, or wanga. The nature of hoodoo or conjure, which is still practiced in some places today, is similarly hard to pin down. Anderson contends that conjure "lacks the developed theology" necessary to make it a religion. Though the practice draws on African, American Indian, and Caribbean religious theologies, conjurers in the United States are likely to be Christians. Whatever religion they may follow, however, conjurers engage in a relationship with the supernatural that Anderson says differs from religious belief. While a conjurer may invoke the name of God in casting a spell, she also relies heavily of the powers attributed to roots, feathers, hair, and blood in rendering the spell successful.

According to Anderson, "Nineteenth-century hoodoo was a result of . . . the mixing of multiple African, European and Native American cultures, which together resulted in a form of magic unique to the American South." Anderson maintains that hoodoo originated in sub-Saharan Africa, "where magic has long been a feature of everyday life." The foundation of hoodoo came to the United States with African slaves. Slaves and their owners often lived and worked in close proximity to one another and, over time, they exchanged traditions of religion and culture. Through this exchange, hoodoo absorbed ideas related to European witchcraft, folk remedies, and the pseudo-science of alchemy. The institution of slavery also brought about intermarriage and the exchange of cultural ideas between African Americans and American Indians. This was possible because Indian people not only sometimes owned slaves, but they were sometimes held as slaves. From American Indian traditions, hoodoo absorbed the traditions of ceremonies, medicine bundles, and herbalism.[7]

It is likely that conjure made its way to Missouri in the eighteenth century with African American slaves who were imported into the territory to work in lead mines and the fields. Slaves were often shipped to Missouri on the Mississippi River, through the port of New Orleans, which was long a stronghold of hoodoo tradition. Because of its strong slave-holding culture, Missouri was home to an active community of hoodoo practitioners, and Owen was able to find several conjurers living in and around St. Joseph in the late 1880s and early 1890s.[8]

Within a few weeks of receiving her first letter from Leland, Owen undertook the earliest fieldwork that she conducted in the name of professional folklore. On July 1, 1889, Owen, in the company of a group of friends that included her sister-in-law Harriet Kearny Owen, visited a well-known conjurer who went by the name of King Alexander. She had long known about King Alexander, who was of mixed African American and Cherokee ancestry, but because of his transient lifestyle, she had never before been able to locate him. On the day Owen met him, he had just returned to St. Joseph from a trip to Boone County, Missouri. In recounting their initial meeting, Owen did not even attempt to conceal the distain she felt upon finally laying eyes on the great conjurer. When the party arrived at the house where he was staying, they found him in what Owen described as a most "unkingly state," sitting on the front porch dressed in a torn shirt and ill-fitting trousers. "As I looked at him," she later wrote, "I thought, 'Well, you are the most uncanny old nigger I ever saw'; as I drew nearer, I added, 'and the dirtiest.'"[9]

King Alexander seems to have been equally unimpressed with the affluent white women who stood before him in the hot July sun. Harriet Owen told him that they had come to buy some "jack," or luck, to which King Alexander replied that he was a church member and knew nothing of such things. "Go 'long ladies," he said. "I ain't de one you a huntin'." In an effort prevent the conjurer from dismissing them, Mary Owen informed him that she practiced some hoodoo herself. "I can make a trick of stump-water, grave-dust, jay feathers, and baby fingers that can strike like lightning," she told King Alexander. Owen reported that this declaration of her familiarity with the practice changed the conjurer's attitude toward them and they made an appointment with him to buy the desired luck charm.[10]

Two days later, King Alexander came to the Owen home. According to Mary, "he drank a good deal of whiskey, sang songs, told rabbit, bird, and ghost stories, assured me I was strong enough in the head to make a good Voodoo, [and] boasted extravagantly of his power over the fair sex."[11] In between, King Alexander made a luck ball for Charles Leland. According to Jeffrey Anderson, luck balls "did more than communicate luck in the European sense; they also embodied the souls of their possessors. Their proprietors carried them always, fed them, and spoke to them, calling them by their own names. The loss of one was a dreadful occurrence." As a child, Owen had seen Mymee Whitehead make such fetishes, and in her book *Old Rabbit, the Voodoo, and Other Sorcerers* Owen described Whitehead's panic at temporarily losing her own luck ball: "She ran hither and thither, looking in all possible and impossible places of concealment and obstinately refusing to state what she had lost. Finally, with a groan of despair, she flung herself down on her cabin floor in a cowering heap and quavered out that she would be better off in her grave, for an enemy had stolen her luck-ball, and her soul as well as her luck was in it." In the book, the story ended happily as Owen's alter ego, Tow Head, found the ball by Whitehead's bed and returned it, much to Whitehead's relief.[12]

As King Alexander crafted Leland's luck ball, Owen took detailed notes that she would later use to recreate the scene in *Old Rabbit*. While Whitehead had made luck balls with the wing of a jaybird, jaw of a squirrel, rattlesnake fang, dust from a grave, and blood from a pig, Owen reported that King Alexander made Leland's luck fetish with red clover, dust, tinfoil, white yarn, white sewing silk, and whiskey. When he began to chant under his breath, Owen interjected, "Stop! Stop! You are not dealing fairly with me. You promised that I should hear your incantation, and you mumble so that I cannot distinguish a word." King Alexander humored Owen in the beginning by chanting out loud:

> The God before me, God behind me, God be with me. May this ball bring all good luck to Charles Leland. May it bind down all devils, may it bind down his enemies before him, may it bring them under his feet. May it bring him friends in plenty, may it bring him faithful friends, may it bind them to him. May it bring him honor, may it bring him riches, may it bring him his heart's desire. May it bring him success in everything he undertakes. May it bring him happiness. I call for it in the Name of God."

Eventually, King Alexander simply waved his hand dismissively at Owen and completed the bundle while chanting under his breath.[13]

Leland was ecstatic, both with the fetish Owen sent him and the information she reported that she was gaining from her interviews with King Alexander. "Cherish your old negro as you would a grandfather," he advised her in a letter. "You are in a rich field and must cultivate it."[14] Leland giddily reported to Owen that the luck ball worked "the most delightful miracles" as he and his wife traveled from Stockholm to England in October 1889. Tickets to overbooked sleeping cars suddenly became available to them, a lost diamond was found and an old acquaintance unexpectedly appeared, all because Leland claimed to have invoked the spirit of the charm. "As for my little spirit, I can only say, Blessings on him and on her who sent him to me."[15]

There is little doubt that Leland had a significant influence over Owen's career, especially in the first few years of their correspondence. Unfortunately, none of the letters Owen wrote to Leland between 1889 and 1893 are known to have survived. However, the letters she sent him after 1893 reveal that she possessed both a professional admiration and a dogged loyalty to her mentor. She often seemed in awe of the fact that a person of Leland's professional distinction chose to correspond with her, and she closed nearly all of her letters by reminding him that she was his "faithful follower." Leland's letters from the early years of their correspondence show that Owen often expressed her esteem for him—and perhaps sought his approval—by sending him an assortment of unusual gifts befitting of an eminent folklorist. He was especially fond of a black conjurer's stone, which Owen gave him when they met face-to-face for the first time in 1891. "There are altogether in all America only 5 or 6 conjurin' stones, small black pebbles, which come from Africa," Leland bragged in a letter to a relative. "Whoever owns one becomes thereby a chief Voodoo—all the years of fasting, ceremonies, etc., can be dispensed with. Miss Owen found one out and promised it. The one who had it would not sell it, so she—stole it. . . . And then gave it to me."[16]

Owen reported that conjurer's stones were very valuable because they held all of the secrets of hoodoo. "Nothing is required of him who holds it," she wrote. The stone "is initiation, it is knowledge, it is power. . . . They are said to have been brought from Africa (or the 'outlandish country,' as the negroes call it), and are handed down through families as their most precious possessions." It appears that the stone had been stolen, though Owen stopped short of admitting that she had been the one responsible for taking it, saying only that it "fell into" her hands. She justified the theft of the stone by reporting that its "unworthy owner" had been "a dissipated and malicious negro, who practiced on the superstitions of his race that he might live in a brutish and debased idleness."[17]

With King Alexander's assistance and Leland's encouragement, Owen spent much of 1890 and 1891 immersed in the world of hoodoo. After their initial meetings, King Alexander promised to find Owen a conjurer with whom she could study. That teacher was a woman Owen called Aunt Dorcas. She described Aunt Dorcas as "a little, lame, poverty-stricken old black woman, whose ability to 'fetch luck' evidently did not extend to herself." Owen recalled that she first met Aunt Dorcas when she walked "up to me in a butcher-shop, and, taking me on one side under pretence of asking for work, told me of the initiation of leaves."[18] The initiation of the leaves was part of Owen's induction into the ways of conjuring. When explaining the ritual later, Owen quoted Aunt Dorcas directly:

> "Go at midnight to a fallow field, go bare-footed, bare-headed, walking backward, and not looking on the ground. Stoop down in the field, reach your hand behind you, and pull up a weed by the roots. Run home, fling the weed under your bed, and leave it there until sunrise. At sunrise strip off its leaves, make them into a little packet, and wear it under your right arm for nine days. At the close of the ninth day, take the packet, separate the leaves and scatter them to the four winds of heaven, throwing them, a few at a time, over your right shoulder as you turn round and round, so as to have them fall east, south, west, and north. What dreams you have during the nine days are warnings, consequently you must carefully consider the 'sign' of them. For instance, if you dream of fire you will have trouble in getting your witch education. If you dream of honey bees you will be a successful conjurer, and receive money and presents. As soon as your leaves are scattered you are ready for lessons."[19]

Owen reported that her lessons included a season spent learning about herbs, vegetable remedies, and poisons. "There is nothing mysterious in this much of the profession," she later recalled. "Any old woman who has an herb-bag has the same samples as a witch." Another early lesson required her to learn the importance of "Luck Numbers." According to King Alexander, "seven is a lucky number to conjure or hoodoo by," she wrote, "but nine is better; three is a good number, but five is better. Four times four is the Great Number. Neither the devil nor his still greater wife can refuse to assist in the working of a charm with that number 'quoted in.'"[20]

Owen's next lesson in hoodoo was to learn the four degrees of charms and fetishes. The first and most difficult degree of charms was related to those that were designed to do good, such as luck balls, or "jack." These were the hardest, reported Owen, because it is always more difficult to do good than it is to do evil. The second class of charms was made in the name of the devil. As Owen put it, "those queer little linen, woolen, or fur bags, or tiny bottles filled with broken glass, bits of flannel, hair, ashes, alum, grave-dust, jay or whippoorwill feathers, bits of bone, parts of snakes, toads, newts, squirrels, fingers of strangled babes and frog-legs." Charms of the third class contained body parts, such as hair, fingernails, saliva, teeth and scabs. These were used in conjunction with other items to do either good or evil. In explaining these charms to Owen, King Alexander told her, "I could save or ruin you if I could get hold of so much as one eye-winker or the peeling of one freckle." The final degree of charms was made up of various simple objects that could be "commanded" to do things. King Alexander used the locust thorn to illustrate. It can be "used innocently enough as a hairpin or dress-fastener, but which when 'commanded' proves a terrible little engine of mischief."[21]

In all, Owen claimed to have interviewed more than twenty conjurers by the summer of 1891. She wrote about Arthur McManus, a sixty-five-year-old conjurer from Kentucky whom her sister-in-law, Harriet Owen was able to locate in St. Joseph. "He [is] certainly is the worst rogue I ever met," Owen wrote. "He is a mulatto, and terribly crippled . . . but he says he was conjured by Mandy Jones," another hoodoo practitioner.[22]

Owen also traveled to the nearly town of Plattsburg, Missouri, to visit Ellen Merida, whom she described as "an enormously fat yellow woman, with a cracked soprano voice and a husky laugh" who "greeted me effusively." Like King Alexander, Merida initially refused to acknowledge that she was a conjurer, especially when curious neighbors stopped by to be introduced to Merida's white visitor. When Owen grew frustrated over her inability to gather the information she wanted, Merida took her to another room and told her to come back when the moon was full or a little past full. "That's the time for cunjerin'," she told Owen. "It's too early in the month now."[23]

King Alexander, Arthur McManus, Mandy Jones, and another of Owen's informants, a man named John Palmer, were all part of a group that Owen referred to in her writing as the Voodoo Circle, or simply the "Circle." The Circle, explained Owen, was "a society for the dissemination of knowledge, and the trial of strength." Palmer offered to take Owen to a meeting, but it is unclear whether she accepted. In St. Joseph, Circle meetings were held at an African Methodist Church late on nights when the moon was dark. Owen wrote that at the meetings, members "talk of their own and one another's exploits, and give and receive news of the Voodoos scattered from New York to Florida." Owen reported that, while the Circle was not a hierarchical organization, there seemed to be a pecking order of sorts, which was based on the ability of members to exert their will upon one another. She believed that King Alexander was the self-appointed leader of the St. Joseph Circle—there were apparently circles all over the nation—and McManus was the "second in importance."[24]

During one meeting in May 1891, Owen learned that the members of the Circle entertained themselves by "willing" each other. "One man would stand in the front of the building and will one from the group at the back to come to him. By turns, everyone except Alexander was willed from his place."[25] Owen came to believe that the assertion of willpower and the ability to control others was hoodoo's defining element. When asked to describe hoodoo at a folklore conference in Chicago, she replied, "It is hypnotism, it is telepathy, it is clairvoyance—in a word, it is WILL." She continued by stating that the conjurer's motto was "control yourself perfectly and you can control the rest of the world—organic and inorganic."[26]

Owen found some of the ceremonies she witnessed in her fieldwork as a hoodoo apprentice to be distasteful, and she refused to attend dances because she feared for her safety. She wrote about the various dances that conjurers held on the outskirts of St. Joseph in an African American suburb known as Africa, or in the surrounding countryside. While the dances were related to hoodoo, she said not everyone who attended was a conjurer. Sometimes they were held at the end of camp revival meetings "after the preachers and more respectable attendants left." She portrayed the dances as rowdy affairs filled with violence, wild movements, and animal sacrifices, yet she admitted that she had never "had but a glimpse of a dance, and that was when a child." In the course of her fieldwork, she generally heard about dances after they happened, emphatically stating that she "certainly would not have risked my life by attending if I had been invited." Owen reported that stabbings and shootings were common at such events, though she declared that, when it came to learning what really happened at the dances, she was skeptical about "the testimony of those old rascals who have instructed me." When asked why she couldn't get a male friend to attend dances to gather information for her, she replied that she could not find a man who would even consider it. "Peril life and reputation among those beasts?" exclaimed one male friend. "Not I! It will be better for the world when they and all knowledge of their vileness die out."[27]

Owen wrote disparagingly about what she characterized as the conjurers' frequent use of whiskey and tobacco. She reported that it was common for students and teachers of hoodoo to get drunk during their lessons and hastened to add that on that point, she "was an honorable exception to the rule," though she did consent to providing whisky for informants during her interviews with them.[28] As we have already seen, Owen often expressed her repulsion at the personal appearance and conduct of some of her informants and while she was fascinated with hoodoo on an intellectual level, she tended to be highly critical of its practitioners. When speaking to an audience of folklorists in 1891, for example, she described conjurers by saying,

> How *could* I describe . . . the cunning, simple, cruel, kindly, untruthful, suspicious yet credulous, superstitious negro, who sees a ghost or devil in every black stump and swaying bush, yet prowls about two-thirds of the night and sleeps three-fourths of the day. The old-fashioned negro, who is destined to have no son like him, who conjures in the name of his African devil on Saturday, and goes to a Christian church, sings, prays, and exhorts, and after "meetin'" invites the minister to a dinner of stolen poultry on Sunday.[29]

Owen assured her audience that even though she was a white woman, she was uniquely qualified to render accurate descriptions of her informants because she had lived among African Americans all her life and was one of the few who understood "our Americanized African population." However, it is clear that Owen's understanding of hoodoo, conjurers, and African Americans in general was clouded with the sort of overt racism that was prevalent among whites in the late nineteenth century.

As a white woman of affluent means, Owen had indeed lived her entire life with African Americans, but she had never known them as equals. In her world, African Americans had always been either her slaves or servants, and it was Owen's role to instruct, supervise, and, if she thought necessary, admonish them in order to see that they completed the various household tasks that she assigned them. In her letters to Charles Leland, Owen sometimes complained about the difficulty she and her sisters had in managing their African American household servants in what she once referred to as "Nigger-Land." "Yesterday morning we arose and found that everyone of our flock of blackbirds was gone. We telephoned to a caterer for temporary assistance and then to the jail to learn if our domestics had been 'run in' for some trifle such as using a razor on a fellow—man or woman, or stealing somebody's chickens. The latter was the offense. We lock them out of the house at night; you know, so we don't know what goes on from dusk till dawn."[30]

On another occasion, Owen complained to Leland about being disturbed by her African American cook. "I must go to the kitchen and suppress our new cook (another nigger, after all). He is singing 'Death comes a riding on a pale white hoss' till the whole house rings with it."[31] Her low opinion of African Americans was not confined to those who worked for her. Owen once commented to Leland, for example, that she believed they reproduced too freely. "The darkey crop seemed thriving," she wrote. "Every mammy had one pickaninny or two on her back or in her arms."[32] Like many of her white contemporaries, Owen seemed to believe blacks to be inherently lazy, ignorant, and immoral.

Owen's views of African American conjurers were even more severe and were compounded by the fact that she believed that those who believed in hoodoo were among the most superstitious and therefore the most ignorant members of their race. Again, Owen was not alone in her opinions. In his study of conjure in African American society, Jeffrey E. Anderson points out that in postbellum America, conjuring was an embarrassment to those African Americans who were trying to lift the race out of poverty and oppression. The practice was condemned by both whites and blacks who believed that conjure's reliance on superstation was preventing black people from making the progress they needed to assimilate into American society. "Conjure doctors are not so numerous now as they were before our race became so enlightened, but still they are numerous," stated one letter to the editor in the Hampton Institute's African American publication the *Southern Workman* in the late 1870s. "They are a curse to their race."[33]

Owen's writings reveal her revulsion at what she believed to be the heathenish and superstitious nature of conjure. Nothing expresses this conviction more dramatically than the fact that she felt no remorse over the theft of the conjuring stone that she gave to Charles Leland. In writing, Owen chastised the stone's original owner for being "malicious" and judged him to be an "unworthy owner" because she suspected that he preyed "on the superstitions of his race that he might live in a brutish and debased idleness."[34] According to historian David Murray, Owen's attitudes are not particularly surprising. "The idea that 'primitive' people believed in magic and superstition . . . played an important part in maintaining the hierarchies of race."[35]

While Owen's racism taints her writings about hoodoo, she was hardly unique among folklorists of her time. As Murray has observed, "Owen's work reflects the impulse of much of the [late nineteenth-century] folklore world in its combination of genuinely useful information about conjure practice . . . with racist pigeon holing." Catherine Yronwode, author of two books on hoodoo and the proprietor of a magic store, Lucky Mojo Curio Company, and the related web site, LuckyMojo.com, agrees. She finds Owen's description of King Alexander's conjuring of Charles Leland's luck ball to be racist and offensive but believes it is generally an accurate account of the "practices and customs of the African-American South during the 19th century (albeit not always with complete understanding).[36]

Owen's hoodoo fieldwork was interrupted for a time by the death of her father on May 3, 1890. Illness had confined James Owen to his home for several months, so it is likely that Mary and her sisters Luella and Juliette devoted much of their time to helping their mother care for him. "It is truly with grief I learn that a great loss has befallen you," Charles Leland wrote to Mary Owen after learning of the death in July. After expressing his condolences, however, Leland warned her that giving in to her grief was only likely to invite more misery. "Melancholy becomes a kind of painful indulgence, and finally a deadly habit. Work is the great remedy." Leland advised his protégé to "keep up your heart, work hard, live in hope, write books, make a name, study—there is a great deal in you."[37]

And work she did. With the death of their father, Owen and her siblings assumed responsibility for the family's business affairs. While Herbert Owen took charge of the family finances, Mary Owen helped to make sure that their various rental properties were maintained and leased. In her letters to Leland, she mentioned her concern about their rental income and told him that she had learned at least a dozen minstrel songs from Jim Churchill, a singer turned house painter whom she hired on occasion to "'beautify' our tenements between occupancies."[38]

The lives of the Owen siblings were further complicated by the fact that their mother, Agnes Owen, became bedridden after her husband died. Some have speculated that she assumed the role of invalid in order to ensure that her daughters continued to live at home, but Mary Owen's letters reveal that by the mid-1890s, her mother was indeed in a fragile state. "Mother is inclined to take life soberly," she wrote to Leland in 1895, "partly because she has suffered from many bereavements, partly because of her delicate health." Mary, Luella, and Juliette would spend the next two decades caring for their invalid mother. The women's travel schedules became busier as their professional lives flourished. Nonetheless, the sisters remained devoted to their mother and juggled their research and work to make sure that there was always someone at home to be with her.[39]

Despite her new responsibilities, Mary Owen quickly returned to her writing desk. Prior to her father's illness, she had published one of the hoodoo stories she had collected, "Ole Rabbit an' de dawg he stole," in the April 1890 issue of the *Journal of American Folk-Lore*, and she had begun working on the manuscript for her first book. The book was to be a collection of the many hoodoo-related folktales she had learned from Mymee Whitehead, King Alexander, and the other conjurers with whom she worked. These stories, which

Agnes Jeanette Cargill Owen, c. 1890. Agnes Owen was just thirteen years old when she arrived in the newly formed village of St. Joseph in 1843 and only seventeen when she married James Owen in 1848. While her husband was busy with business affairs in the boom years of the 1850s and again during tumultuous years of the Civil War, Agnes Owen acted as a stabilizing force in the Owen household. She educated her children at home after violence closed local schools, teaching them to be independent and self-reliant. (Courtesy of the Missouri State Archives)

featured animals such as Rabbit, Woodpecker, Snake, and the Bee-King, were interspaced with songs, rhymes, and Owen's account of King Alexander making Charles Leland's luck ball. To tie the stories together, Owen included five characters, Aunt Mymee, Aunt Mary, Big Angy, Aunt Em'ly, and Granny, that took turns spinning tales for young Tow Head, the character that Owen used as her alter ego.

By July, Owen had begun sending chapters of her manuscript to Leland for his comments. Though he was pleased with the initial chapters, Leland expressed several concerns about the project. Most significantly, he worried that a collection of African American animal stories would inevitably be compared to the popular Uncle Remus plantation stories that Joel Chandler Harris had begun publishing more than a decade earlier. Indeed there were similarities. By the time the first Uncle Remus book was published in 1880, Chandler had developed the character of an elderly slave as a literary device. Using Uncle Remus to tell stories to a little boy allowed Chandler the opportunity to present the tales in a unified manner, much as Owen had done by using the characters of five African American women and the young girl named Tow Head.

Leland advised Owen that it would be better if white Missouri peasants told the stories in the book. While he did not elaborate on his reasons for this suggestion, it may have had to do with his concerns over Owen's use of black dialect, a device that Chandler had also used in the Uncle Remus stories. While the use of dialect is considered racist today, Leland objected to dialect simply because it made the stories difficult to read. "Remember that your Missouri negro-English is *difficult* for many Americans to understand, and almost a foreign tongue to English readers," he warned her. "Be liberal with translations."[40]

Leland advised Owen to "call earnest attention to the fact that your work differs much from the Brer Rabbit stories," adding that she should be clear that the book was a "collection of Folk-Lore, and that it is not intended to be merely a story book." In fact, Chandler also claimed that the Uncle Remus stories were folklore and that he had recorded them as mere transcriptions of stories he had heard from African American sources. Referring to himself as an "accidental author," he denied any literary motivations behind the work. This, however, does not appear to have been true. Jay Hansford C. Vest, who is a scholar of indigenous religion and oral tradition, has shown that Chandler received his stories from a variety of sources, many of which were not African American. On at least one occasion, Chandler placed an advertisement in a Georgia newspaper asking readers to send him fables. Chandler also admitted to writing multiple drafts of his stories and, according to Vest, showed a willingness to alter his stories to conform to the tastes and expectations of his white audience.[41]

Charles Leland also suggested that Owen point out to her readers that the tales in her manuscript were as closely connected to the traditions of American Indians as they were to African Americans. While Leland and Owen saw the similarities, they, like most scholars of their time, believed that Indians had learned the stories from African Americans. Vest points out that animal stories like the ones Owen and Chandler published probably originated with American Indians. For instance, stories featuring trickster rabbits similar to Chandler's Brer Rabbit and Owen's Old Rabbit were not only told widely in Indian cultures across the continental United States, they appeared as far away as the Amazon region of South America. Vest believes that Native Americans developed these stories, which also feature such animal characters as wolves, wildcats, and bears, out of their centuries-long familiarity with the North American ecology. Indians knew these animals well, while African Americans generally did not. Not only were there no African equivalents to some of the animals featured in these stories, writes Vest, but the confined manner in which slaves were forced to live prevented African Americans from acquiring a wide cultural familiarity with the wildlife in this hemisphere. "It is simply illogical to assume," writes Vest, "that African slaves would choose wild animals . . . with which they had little or no familiarity to be their folk-motif characters."

Despite these concerns, Leland praised Owen's efforts overall and offered to write an introduction for the book. "Even if this work could not be published . . . it would be a great triumph to have written it. It is replete with shrewd observations of folk-lore, it is inspired with real humor, it is concise and strong. So God bless it and you, and may you both 'Go It!'"[42] Indeed, Leland must have been proud of Owen's work, because he invited her to submit a proposal to present a paper at the Second International Folk-Lore Congress, which was to be held in London the next year. The following months were surely busy ones for Owen as she juggled her family duties with the demands of preparing her first book for publication and writing the first presentation she would ever give in front of an audience of professional folklorists.

Five

"A Folklorist Born, Not Made," 1891–1895

As Mary Alicia Owen and other folklorists from around the world prepared for the Second International Folk-Lore Congress to open in October 1891—the first congress had taken place in Paris in 1889—many were concerned that the discipline stood at an academic crossroads. While the study of folklore has been traced back to the Brothers Grimm and their collection of fairy tales, which first appeared in 1812, the term "folklore" did not appear until 1846. Writing in the magazine *Athenaeum*, British writer William John Thoms proposed the term folklore as the "lore of the people," which he said included such things as manners, customs, observances, superstitions, ballads, and proverbs.[1] For decades, the discipline had been the domain of amateurs who collected curiosities from a variety of cultures and who possessed little regard for academic rigor or analysis. By the 1880s, as folklorists sought to legitimize their discipline through professionalism and scientific investigation, they found themselves splitting into two broad theoretical camps. The anthropological school believed that the key to understanding folklore was to be found in the study of the culture from with it came, while the literary school argued that folklore should be analyzed separately from the culture that created it.

The so-called literary school's belief that mythology, folk songs, and oral tradition should be collected and scientifically analyzed without regard for the people that produced them grew out of the theory of social evolution. Social evolution claimed that all of the world's societies shared similar beginnings and followed the same trajectory of development. While the literary school acknowledged that not all societies were alike, they attributed any differences to the belief that some groups of people, such as African Americans and American Indians, had simply advanced more slowly than others. Folklorists of the literary school found these societies to be of particular interest because they theorized that their so-called primitive ways were remnants of the ancient past that all people shared.

Adam Smith and members of the Scottish Enlightenment had pioneered ideas about social evolution in the eighteenth century. They put forth the theory that all societies passed through the same four stages of development: the Age of Hunters, the Age of Shepherds, the Age of Agriculture, and the Age of Commerce.[2] Edward B. Tylor, the first anthropologist and folklorist in Britain to occupy a university faculty position, built upon this idea in his 1871 book *Primitive Cultures*. In the book, Tylor argued that all societies began at the lowly state of primitive savagery, or "animism," and evolved slowly toward a state of civilization. Tylor believed that it was possible to chart the path of that progress through the study of certain cultural remnants, which he called "survivals." Survivals were things like myths, riddles, games, and material culture, which Tylor believed were evidence of a culture's ancient, less-civilized past. According to historian Stephen K. Sanderson, survivals did not make sense in the modern world because they "had been carried on by force of habit into a new state of society different from that in which they had their original home." However, because survivals were relics of the past, Tylor believed that a scientific understanding of them would allow nineteenth-century social scientists to catch a glimpse of the ancient primitive past that all modern people had in common.[3]

The American anthropologist Lewis Henry Morgan further refined the idea of social evolution in his 1877 book *Ancient Society*. Morgan stated, "All the facts of human knowledge and experience tend to show that the human race, as a whole, has steadily progressed from a lower to a higher condition."[4] He mapped the stages through which he believed cultures passed as they progressed from their primitive beginnings toward civilization. He divided the process of social evolution into three main stages: savagery, barbarianism, and civilization. In the state of savagery, subsistence was limited to hunting and gathering. As societies acquired the use of weapons and the ability to make pottery, they transitioned into the state of barbarianism. In this phase, humans began to gain mastery over their environment by domesticating animals, designing irrigation systems, and, finally, learning to work with metal. As societies developed writing, they entered the phase of civilization in which they also developed civil government and the concept of individual property.[5]

The literary folklorists' interpretation of the theory of social evolution led them to define "folk" as people whose primitive ways had made them unable to participate in contemporary society at large. They lumped gypsies, peasants, American Indians, and African Americans into this category and scanned their folk traditions for survivals. Unlike the amateurs of a generation earlier, literary folklorists tended to specialize in collecting particular kinds of folklore, such as songs, nursery rhymes, or games. Yet they tended to collect these tidbits from a broad spectrum of cultures in an attempt to discover commonalities that would lead them back to the very beginnings of European culture.[6]

The anthropological school employed the theory of social evolution somewhat differently in their study of folklore. While the literary school believed that "folk" were marginalized members of mainstream society, the anthropological school defined folk as those people who lived in small societies that were not directly related to modern Western culture. They understood that these societies had developed separately from mainstream European society and realized that these separate societies practiced their own traditions and had their own cultures. Consequently, anthropological folklorists believed that such cultural fragments as ceremonies, songs, and oral traditions were not remnants of the ancient beginnings of European American tradition. Instead, they understood these things to be unique expressions of the people who made them. As such, they saw folklore as an important key to understanding specific cultures.[7]

Many members of the anthropological school understood social evolution in terms of Charles Darwin's theory of "survival of the fittest." Just as organisms in the natural world must adapt to the conditions of their environment in order to survive, so too must cultures. Social scientists of the Victorian era widely believed that certain cultures were in danger of vanishing forever because they had not managed to keep pace with the rapidly changing nature of contemporary society. They believed that American Indians in particular were destined to vanish because they had become stuck in a primitive past that prevented them from functioning in the modern world. For this reason, Indians, along with other supposedly primitive cultures, became the focus of intensive study in the hopes that much of their folklore and culture could be preserved before they disappeared.

The American Folklore Society, founded in Cambridge, Massachusetts in 1888, became a strong advocate of the anthropological school. Writing in the first issue of the *Journal of American Folklore*, the society's president William Wells Newell called for the "collection of the fast-vanishing remains of Folk-Lore in America." His list of endangered folklore included that of the Old English, African Americans, American Indians, French Canadians, and Mexicans. He expressed his belief in the importance of the comprehensive study of native cultures in order to better understand them. "It does not appear either desirable or possible, in dealing with a primitive people," he wrote, "to include a part and exclude another part of its traditions." He vowed that the *Journal of American Folklore* would uphold this model of folklore scholarship in the articles that it published.[8]

This debate over theory and the future of folklore studies set the stage for the Second International Folk-Lore Congress, which was to open in London on Thursday, October 1. The September 1891 issue of the British journal *Folk-Lore* announced that plans for the weeklong congress were set and that the success of the meeting was guaranteed. While this was to be the first gathering of British folklorists, *Folk-Lore* noted that the conference would live up to its claim to be an international meeting as folklorists from the United States, France, Finland, and Germany were expected to attend. The planning committee took pains to balance the social aspects of the meeting with the important scientific work that they hoped to highlight there. "For the first time since the science [of folklore] has taken a position among the organized methods of studying the past," reported the journal, "its adherents meet for the purpose of becoming known to one another and putting their heads together to discover the best methods of promoting their favorite study."[9]

The international congress was to be divided into three parts: the folktale section, the mythological section, and the institutional section. Each section would convene for one of the meeting's six days. There was also to be a trip to Oxford and the British Museum, an evening "conversazione" that would include demonstrations of a mummers' play, a sword dance, "savage" music, and children's games played by students from a nearby village school. Throughout the congress, there would be exhibits of such curiosities as a "Japanese shrine for domestic worship," various charms and amulets, a collection of shepherd's crooks, and a number of harvest dolls known as Kern babies.[10]

Mary Alicia Owen's presentation was part of the mythological section, which met at the Society of Antiquaries in Burlington House on October 5. In his remarks at the opening of the session, John Rhys, professor of Celtic studies at Oxford University and a member of the literary school, expressed his conviction that there was great promise in the comparative study of mythology across cultures. "One might," he theorized, "compare the myths of Greeks, and Teutons, and Hindoos, because those nations were admitted to be of the same stock." He lamented that many folklorists seemed timid in undertaking such comparative analysis and members of the anthropological school were making too much out of the study of culture as it related to folklore.[11]

Of the speakers who followed Rhys that day, three spoke from a literary point of view. The French folklorist Charles Ploix delivered a paper on the myth of *The Odyssey*, in which he compared Ulysses to the heroes of European folktales, *J. S. Stuart Glennie* spoke about the origins of mythology, and Edward B. Tylor read a paper he had written about charms and instruments of sorcery. Somewhat less literary in perspective was Charles Leland's discussion about his research into the practice of witchcraft, which he said had once prevailed among certain cults in Tuscany.

Perhaps because he represented an older generation of amateur folklorists, Leland distrusted theories and had little patience for those who promoted them, whom he chastised for being "men of books and not of the folk."[12] Though he may not have been willing to admit it, he did share the literary school's interest in survivals and their importance in uncovering the common origins of various cultures. Leland placed great importance on gathering folklore from living informants and showed a particular interest in English gypsies and Etruscan witches. Folklore historian Richard M. Dorson writes, "All the folk groups whom Leland cultivated seemed to him facets of the same primitive type. The Indians, living in the fields and woods, reminded him of the Gypsies, and so did the Florentine witches, both maintaining the occult practices of an ancient past."[13] No doubt that was what intrigued Leland about Owen's work among the conjurers in Missouri. Like many folklorists of the era, he considered African Americans to be one step closer to the primitive past than whites, and he believed the practice of hoodoo provided a window into those long-gone days and possessed possible connections to the magic he studied in Europe.

Like her mentor, Mary Owen disliked folklore theory. "People interest me in a way that theories do not," she would write in a letter to Leland in 1893.[14] Perhaps it was this self-professed love of people that would lead her to share Leland's interest in collecting folklore firsthand from conjurers, gypsies, and American Indians. However, because she pushed this aspect of her work farther than did Leland, and because she was generally uninterested in making comparisons between the rituals and ceremonies of different cultures, Owen's work tended to be more in line with the anthropological method of study.

In her first folklore conference appearance ever, Owen read a paper in which she discussed her immersion in hoodoo and discussed her encounters with King Alexander, Mymee Whitehead, Arthur McManus, John Palmer, and the other Missouri conjurers with whom she had worked. She gave detailed accounts of the various phases of hoodoo initiation, the workings of the Circle, and even mentioned that she had brought the stolen black conjurer stone to England with her to present to Leland. The *Times* of London, which devoted a generous amount of coverage to the proceedings of the mythological session, reported on Owen's talk in some detail, reporting that she was "alone among white women" in having been initiated into mysteries of voodoo.[15]

After the congress, Leland enthusiastically lauded Owen for the hands-on manner in which she approached her subject. "There were a hundred in the Congress," he wrote later in a letter to his brother-in-law, "and Mary Owen, and [Hugh] Nevill, and Professor [Alfred Cort] Haddon, and I were really *all* the people in it who knew anything about Folk-Lore at *first hand* among niggers, Romany's, Dutch Uncles, hand-organ men, Injuns, bar-maids, tinkers, etc. . . . But Mary takes the rag of all, for she was born to it in wild Missouri."[16] Leland was not alone in his appreciation of the woman from "wild Missouri." Her fellow conference delegates bestowed upon her an honorary membership in the British Folk-Lore Congress and British Association for the Advancement of Science.[17]

As a woman, Owen was not alone in folklore circles. At the turn of the twentieth century, women were beginning to make a significant impact in folklore. While just 10 percent of the members of the Folklore Society were women in 1889, their ranks would swell to 37 percent of its membership by 1910. Measured by this standard, women participated more in the discipline of folklore than in most other professional or academic fields of the time.[18] Despite the protests of American Folklore Society president Stewart Cullin, who in 1897 would warn that folklore was too "rough edged" for women, collecting stories and documenting folkways were generally deemed to be appropriate activities for ladies of the late Victorian Age. Their influence in the study of lore related to plants, animals, children, toys, games, and mythology was so significant in the 1890s that some men feared the discipline was becoming feminized.[19]

However, because Owen came from "wild Missouri," a place that the Europeans still linked to the American frontier, and because she had studied with African American conjurers and watched them practice their magic in person, she had an air of authenticity that was unmatched by other attendees at the London conference. The fact that she had grown up, as Leland put it, "among the most 'superstitious' race conceivable" and that she "alone among white women" had been privileged to learn the dark secrets of hoodoo only enhanced her status as an authority on such matters.

Leland was eager to get Owen's collection of hoodoo stories into print. Two days after he and Owen read their papers at the folklore congress, he wrote to the British publisher Thomas Fisher Unwin to inform him that as soon as the conference was over, he would deliver Owen's manuscript and a contract to Fisher's publishing house in London. He warned Fisher that Owen was still "engaged in making [the manuscript's] nigger English into something more directly intelligible." Nonetheless, he remained optimistic about the likelihood that the manuscript would be approved for publication.

"I think that our good Unwin will take Mary Owen's book," Leland told his brother-in-law in a letter on October 11. "She has been a great success."[20]

After returning home, Owen continued her work on hoodoo and, most likely at Leland's prodding, she planned a second book on the topic. Sometime in the early spring of 1892, however, her primary hoodoo informant King Alexander died. In April, she traveled to Philadelphia for a folklore meeting and, as the year progressed, eagerly anticipated the publication of her first book while planning to attend the third folklore congress, which was to be held in the summer of 1893 in conjunction with the World's Columbian Exposition in Chicago.

T. Fisher Unwin published Owen's *Old Rabbit, the Voodoo, and Other Sorcerers* in London in early 1893. At about the same time, G. P. Putnam's Sons of New York published the book in the United States under the title *Voodoo Tales as Told among the Negroes of the Southwest*. Charles Leland wrote the introduction to the book, which included illustrations by the British illustrator Louis Wain and Mary's sister Juliette. Notices for the publication began to appear in newspapers on the first of April, with the *New York Sun* reproducing four of stories from the book in its April 9 edition. The unnamed reviewer for the *New York Times* was unimpressed with the book and doubted Leland's claim that it was of great use to folklorists. The *Times* questioned Leland's assertion that the stories were the product of a group that shared African American and American Indian ancestry. "These stories, though interesting, are all of too recent manufacture to be of great use in folklore studies. It is the mixing up of the two, which would impair any positive value."[21]

As Leland had expected, reviewers also remarked on the similarity between *Old Rabbit* and the popular *Uncle Remus* books. "The machinery Miss Owen uses bears a strong resemblance to Mr. Joel Chandler's method," wrote the *Times* reviewer, "and in little Tow Head we have the small boy, Miss Sally's child, who draws out from Uncle Remus his wealth of stories." In his review in the journal *Folklore*, E. Sidney Hartland noted, "Usually, the setting of a work on folklore in a fictitious, or semi-fictitious, framework is hardly to be commended from the scientific view." Nonetheless, Hartland believed that in Owen's case, the format worked because the richness with which she described her main characters helped to set the context from which these stories came. Hartland also pointed out that Owen's collection was not "confined to those [stories] with which we are familiar in *Uncle Remus* and Mr. Charles Jones's *Negro Myths from the Georgia Coast*," noting that many of Owen's stories were "quite new." He attributed this to the fact that many were heavily influenced by American Indian traditions. He judged that the relationship of the stories to the traditions and practice of hoodoo would only be determined "when we have a fuller and more systematic account before us." He continued, "Miss Owen was able to only whet our appetite at the London Congress; and she is far from satisfying it on the subject of Voodoo mysteries in *Old Rabbit*."[22]

In the *Journal of American Folklore*, a review written by James Owen Dorsey, a missionary who had spent years studying Siouan languages and tales, also touted the Indian origins of the collection. Dorsey noted, "This is the first indication of the existence, among Missouri negroes, of tales so closely corresponding to Indian narratives." Dorsey believed that most of the stories found in *Old Rabbit* were deeply rooted in American Indian traditions. In support of this point, he carefully noted the similarities between the tales Owen had collected and those told by tribes whose traditional homes had been very near St. Joseph: the Osage, Omaha, Ponca, and Ioway. He regretted that Owen had not been clearer about the specific informants who had provided her with her stories and urged her to continue her work so that in the future "the history of these variants of Indian tales may be traced with exactitude."[23]

If Owen was concerned about the reviews of *Old Rabbit*, there is no record of it. She spent the summer of 1893 preparing for her talk at the upcoming folklore congress in Chicago and working on her second "voodoo book." Writing to Leland in late June, she said that she was "working cheerfully" on the manuscript. "I had about half the thing done when I found that it must all be re-written." While she seemed pleased with her book, she vented her overall frustration with hoodoo, which she felt was a vile practice. "All the fetishes, rubbish and incantations" were designed to scare people, she complained to her mentor. "The real Voodoo of the priests is silent and terrible."[24]

Her contempt for hoodoo and conjurers spilled over into the lecture she was preparing to deliver in Chicago on July 12. In describing a typical conjurer, Owen wrote,

In substantial flesh and almost superhuman power for mischief, he stands, a verity of the present, shoulder to shoulder with
you and me, instantly ready, at the instance of his own hate or
another's hire, to jostle us from our place and despoil us of our
goods and health. Here he is, grinning at conscience, mocking at
law, jeering at all virtues but self-control. Utterly heartless, abnor-
mally conceited, trained by self-torture to the highest pitch of en-
durance, he might be a menace to civilization were there not one
talisman that sends him cowering as did the seal of Solomon.

The "talisman of Solomon" to which Owen referred was the po-
liceman's badge.[25]

Since the folklore congress in London two years earlier, the split
between the literary and anthropological folklorists had reached
such proportions that the two groups planned to hold separate conferences in Chicago in the summer of 1893. Fletcher Bassett, who
had founded the Chicago Folklore Society in 1891, organized the
Third International Folklore Congress, which was to take place the
week of July 10. A strong proponent of literary folklore, Bassett
planned the congress to cover myths and traditional beliefs; oral
literature and folk music; customs, institution and rituals; and artistic, emblematic, and economic folklore. Citing philosophical differences with Bassett and the literary school, the American Folklore
Society declined to support the congress. Because the leaders of the
American Folklore Society believed folklore to be part of the anthropological sciences, they scheduled their meeting to coincide with
the Anthropological Congress, which was to be held at the Columbian Exposition on August 28, 1893.[26]

The anthropological meeting had to be rescheduled at the last
minute—papers were finally presented on August 29 and 31—and
organizers were disappointed at its lack of success. Bassett's folklore
congress, on the other hand, proved to be far more popular. Sixty-
three presenters, four of them women, read papers between July 10
and July 17. In his opening address on July 11, Bassett outlined his
ideas about the importance of folklore in the study of history.[27]

Folklore is not merely a study of the survival of decay, it is the
demonstrator of the possible and probable in history, the reposito-
ry of historical truths otherwise lost, the preserver of the literature
of the people and the touchstone of many of the sciences. History

may lie, tradition never does; literature may claim to have found the new thing under the sun, but comparative Folklore detects the analogies to other creations.[28]

Owen read her paper, titled "Voodooism," the following evening. She shared her session with John Abercromby, who spoke on "The Magic Poetry of the Finns, and Its Application in Practice," and Professor Vulko I. Shopoff, who read a paper on "Bulgarian Wedding Ceremonies." U.S. Army captain H. L Scott discussed "The Sign Language of the Plains Indians," while four Sioux Indians, Flat Iron, Horse-Come-Last, Standing Bear, and Painted Horse, demonstrated sign language for the audience.

In her presentation, Owen read two hoodoo stories, one of them about Old Grandfather Rattlesnake, who King Alexander had told her was the founder of hoodoo. She spoke about the Circle and the conjurers' power of will. "Hypnotism is the Voodoo's pastime, as well as his power," she told her audience.[29] Though Owen provided her audience with a variety of salacious details about hoodoo and the practice of conjuring, she avoided making any claims about the importance of collecting African American folklore or about its value to folklore. That claim was made by another folklorist attending the congress, Annah Robinson Watson, who presented a paper titled "Comparative Afro-American Folk-Lore." "The American Negro is many generations nearer the savage existence than any race—excepting the Indian," Watson told the conference, "His nearness to this primitive state accounts for his rich possession of legends, his dower of heredity accounts for the character of these legends."[30]

On some level, Owen must have agreed with Watson. Owen sometimes expressed opinions about African Americans that indicated that she saw them as being less than her equals. Yet, like Watson, Owen believed African American culture was a rich field of study, and though she found hoodoo and conjurers to be repugnant, she remained determined to collect as many of their stories and witness as many of their rituals as possible.

Unfortunately, Owen was never specific about the reasons for her dogged pursuit of hoodoo folklore. She did not seem to share Leland's interest in finding the commonalities that linked conjuring to the traditions of ritual and magic found in other cultures. It is possible that, like many in the field, Owen saw it as her duty to preserve fragments of what she perceived to be a primitive culture that was doomed to vanish in the modern world. Quite likely, she believed that there would be a time when hoodoo would become a lost art and her writings on the topic would document it for posterity. It is also possible that Owen simply enjoyed hoodoo because of its exotic nature and because it provided her with the opportunity to relay a variety of unique experiences to audiences around the world. She had, after all, spent more than a decade writing fiction and had a connoisseur's appreciation for a good story.

Owen seemed to enjoy being known as a "voodoo" herself, especially when the distinction began to bring her fame. By 1895, she was touted in the popular press for being "Famous in Folklore" and "one of the most famous folklorists in the world." On more than one occasion, strangers had written asking her to either cast or break hoodoo spells. "I am," she told a newspaper reporter, "a folklorist born not made. I live in the finest possible field for folk lore where superstitions black, red, and of a piebald nature abound." She claimed to be the only white voodoo in existence, adding, "Perhaps my being descended from the seventh son of a seventh son has something to do with my so easily winning the confidence of the folk."[31]

What Owen did not tell the reporter, however, was that she had abandoned her research and had stopped writing about hoodoo and conjurers a year earlier. "I am sorry that the Voodoo business is interrupted," Leland had written to Mary upon hearing the news in February 1894, "but a strong will, ingenious trickery and a belief in you will set it all right. . . . You must rehabilitate yourself."[32] For reasons that remain unclear, however, Owen chose not to "rehabilitate" herself, and she appears to have dropped the topic forever. It is likely that King Alexander's death in 1892 made it more difficult for her to retain her connection with the community of conjurers. Despite her disproval of his intemperance and his ragged appearance, he had proven to be a critical contact for her and had introduced her to many other informants. "It was old 'King' Alexander who really taught [Mary] about voodoo," Juliette Owen reported years later.[33]

Jean Fahey Eberle and Doris Land Mueller have both speculated that Owen abandoned her work because of her belief that hoodoo was a dark practice that allowed a few conjurers to manipulate those who believed in their spells. "Mary knew better than Leland that voodoo relies on the horrible and on the subjective iron will," wrote Eberle. "This was of academic interest to Leland and the other folklorists. To Mary it was a reality. She had seen the results of the terror voodoo practitioners struck in their victims." Eberle related an Owen family story about a great-niece who asked Owen about hoodoo in the 1920s. Owen reportedly told the girl that she had written a book on the topic that had included "the symbols and rituals which had such devastating effects on terrified believers. Unwilling to subject any more human beings to such fear," Owen had destroyed the manuscript.[34]

This undocumented fragment of family history would be easy to dismiss were it not for the fact that Owen's own words support it. We recall how Owen had derisively described a typical conjurer to her Chicago audience and that she had called the former owner of the conjuring stone she had stolen for Leland "a dissipated and malicious negro, who practiced on the superstitions of his race that he might live in a brutish and debased idleness." Remember too what she had written to Leland in the summer of 1893: "The real Voodoo of the priests is silent and terrible."[35]

Owen's decision to drop hoodoo as a topic of research may also have come from the fact that she had begun to immerse herself in the folklore of American Indians. She had begun to travel regularly to the Sac and Fox Reservation near Reserve, Kansas, as early as 1881. In the summer of 1894, she made trips to the nearby Kansas reservations of the Potawatomis, Kickapoos, and Ioways to observe their corn dances, which were the precursor to modern-day powwows. "It was a great sight," she told a newspaper reporter.[36] Mary would spend the next several years studying the ceremonies, customs, stories, and material culture of the Sac and Fox and other tribes that lived near St. Joseph. Her pursuit would result in several new articles, two new books, and a new level of fame.

Six

Noble Savages and Ozark Gypsies, 1894–1900

Following her aborted hoodoo project, Mary Alicia Owen spent the better part of a decade focusing her research and writing on the cultures of the American Indian tribes that lived across the Missouri River from St. Joseph in the state of Kansas. This effort resulted in three major works that were published between 1896 and 1909. The first was a novel, *The Daughter of Alouette*, which appeared in 1896. *The Daughter of Alouette* revives some of the themes Owen first explored in her 1889 short story "The Taming of Tarias." The book focuses on the social interactions that took place between members of the various ethnic populations that inhabited western Missouri during the mid-nineteenth century. It was also Mary's first published work in which American Indians played a significant role. Owen's second book about Indians, *Folk-lore of the Musquakie Indians of North America*, published in London in 1904, was more a work of cultural anthropology than one of folklore. It not only related many of the stories and customs that Mary had observed in her years of visiting the Sac and Fox, it also catalogued the more than one hundred Sac and Fox artifacts that she had collected over the years and that she donated to the Folklore Society in Britain in 1901. Owen again shifted her efforts following the publication of *Folk-lore of the Musquakie* by publishing a play titled *The Sacred Council Hills* in 1909. It is a highly stylized melodrama that takes place among the Sac and Fox during their removal from the future site of St. Joseph and the Platte Country in 1837.

Owen wrote these works at a time when readers in the United States and Europe were hungry for popular literature about Native Americans. While Owen was just one of many European American authors who were attempting to satisfy the public's appetite, there were also a number of native people writing their own stories at the end of the nineteenth century. Literary historian Bernd C. Peyer has suggested that the rise of federally operated boarding schools for Indian children in the 1870s contributed to the emergence of a class of what he called Indian intellectuals by 1900. It was from this generation of Anglo-educated Indians that the first native writers emerged. Peyer has observed that these early authors served as cultural informants who described the traditions, religions, and folkways of their tribal cultures for European American audiences.[1]

Among the best known of these writers was Charles Eastman, a physician and promoter of outdoor activity. His most famous book, *Recollections of a Wild Life*, was an autobiographical account of his traditional Santee Sioux childhood in Minnesota and Canada and the journey that led him to his education at Dartmouth. Similarly, Francis La Flesche, who was Omaha, wrote of his early childhood and of his education at a Presbyterian boarding school in present-day Nebraska. Zitkala-Sa, also known as Gertrude Simmons Bonnin, was a Lakota woman who published articles in the *Atlantic* and *Harpers* and produced two collections of American Indian folklore.[2] These native authors, along with others such as Oglala Lakota Luther Standing Bear and E. Pauline Johnson, who was from Canada's Six Nations confederacy, all wrote works that were deeply rooted in their native heritage. While these authors wrote in a wide range of styles, from ethnography (La Flesche) to poetry (Johnson), all functioned as literary cultural guides who endeavored to help their European American readers gain some knowledge and perspective about their American Indian cultures.[3]

The Harvard-educated anthropologist and showman Antonio Apache was one such native cultural guide with whom Mary Owen was personally acquainted. While Apache's ethnic background would become the topic of a minor scandal in 1907—he was alleged to be an African American posing as an Indian—he claimed to be a descendant of the Apache leader Cochise. A public speaker and performer, Apache also developed exhibits to illustrate traditional American Indian life. New York governor Theodore Roosevelt recommended that Apache serve as curator of the American Indian exhibits for the 1901 Pan American Exposition in Buffalo, though it is not clear that he actually held that position. Later, however, in an attempt to give the public an authentic view of Indian life, Apache opened a living Indian village exhibit and attraction in Los Angeles.[4]

In November 1895, Apache visited Owen in St. Joseph. "He brought me a beautiful specimen of Moqui [Hopi] weaving," she told Charles Leland, "but disappointed me, in as much as he was too hoarse to sing." She reported that Apache had promised to "give us all the sacred chants of the Apaches" when he returned for another visit the following spring. She described an Indian game called "Hunting the Buffalo" that Apache had patented and was hoping to manufacture for sale in the future. "He is a wonderful young fellow," Owen wrote, "and has upset all my theories about his people." Just what those theories were, however, she did not say.

Another native cultural guide with whom Owen corresponded was the writer and showman Edward Hoyt, better known as Buckskin Joe. Hoyt was born in Quebec and learned the skills of hunting and trapping from Indians who lived near his home. Though he claimed to be part Indian, there is reason to doubt that he actually was. Hoyt seems to have modeled his colorful career and his physical appearance after the popular showman Buffalo Bill Cody. Like Cody, he served in the military, worked as a lawman and scout, and performed in Wild West shows. After traveling with Pawnee Bill's Wild West Show in the late 1880s, Hoyt briefly managed his own show in the early 1890s. Owen wrote to Hoyt in the late 1890s and asked him to find an eagle's claw that she could give to Charles Leland. "He is sure to do it in time," she wrote Leland. "You can't hurry an Indian, you know, a thousand years is as a day to them and a day is a thousand years. He don't reckon time any more than his creator is supposed to."[5]

During the 1890s, Owen made regular trips to Kansas to visit various Indian communities where she watched their dances, observed their culture, and collected artifacts. It is not known exactly how or when Owen first made contact with members of Indian nations. Jean Fahey Eberle mentions that the African American women who raised Owen first introduced her to Sac and Fox people to whom they were related sometime before the Civil War. Eberle believes that the opening of a bridge across the Missouri River at St. Joseph in 1873 allowed Owen to begin making regular visits to the tribe's Kansas reservation. In a letter that Owen wrote to A. C. Burrill, the curator of the Missouri State Museum, she placed the beginning of her regular visits in the year 1881. "I dare say," she wrote, "I was 100 times among the Musquakie between 1881 and 1898."[6]

From St. Joseph, Owen had easy access to several American Indian communities. In the 1850s, the land across the Missouri River from St. Joseph had been set aside for the Ioway, Potawatomi, Kickapoo, the Delaware (Leni Lanappe), and the Sac and Fox, whom Owen referred to as the Musquakie (today more commonly spelled Meskwaki). By the 1880s, the Delaware had been removed to the Indian Territory, while the Sac and Fox, Ioway, Kickapoo, and Potawatomi remained on reservations that had been dramatically reduced in size. Each of these reservations would have been easy for Owen to reach in less than a day. The most distant of these, the Potawatomi Reservation, was roughly seventy miles from St. Joseph, and in the 1880s it was possible to reach all four reservations by train.

Predictably, an unmarried white woman's visits to these settlements not only worried her family but they became fodder for gossip among St. Joseph's social elite. Eberle writes that Owen's parents found the idea of Mary's visits with the Indians even more unsettling than her visits to St. Joseph's African American neighborhoods. Nevertheless, the young writer persuaded them that the trips were a necessity that allowed her to gather material that she might use in the stories she was writing in the 1880s. In order to quell any hint of impropriety, Owen sometimes asked members of the local chapter of the Social Science Club or her brother Herbert to accompany her on her visits. In the end her parents accepted her travels, though, according to Eberle, Agnes Owen subjected her eldest daughter to a strict cleansing ritual each time she returned home from a visit with the Indians. Jean Fahey Eberle relates a family story that Agnes Owen hung sheets around one of the exterior porches of the house and Mary was ordered to bathe and dress in clean clothes before being allowed to enter the house.[7]

Owen empathized with the native people she visited and once stated that she believed she possessed an "Indian spirit." She claimed to have been adopted by the Sac and Fox tribe and clearly took great delight in the fact that tribal members allowed her to observe ceremonies that Christian missionaries and government Indian agents disapproved of and were then illegal. In her 1931 letter to Burrill, Owen recounted that she had traveled—apparently on more than one occasion—with tribal members to hold ceremonies in remote locations where government officials would not catch them. "I went to dances (how I hate the silly agents who suppressed them!) in Iowa, Kansas, and Indian Territory," she wrote to Burrill. "We were always dodging those white idiots the government sent out. They seemed to think dancing was devil worship." During these trips, Owen collected hundreds of artifacts. Her large collection contained belts, pipes, moccasins, clothing, bags, and weavings.[8]

By the mid-1890s, Owen's collection had caught the attention of various ethnographers, museum curators, and folklorists. In March 1895 she wrote to Leland about her correspondence with John Wesley Powell, a geologist and explorer of the American West who had just become chief of the Smithsonian Institution's Bureau of Ethnography. "I have promised the Smithsonian people to get them some specimens of the work of our Sacs and Kickapoos," she told Leland. "They have fine collections of Sioux and Apache industries, but so very little from my 'cousins' [who] have more skill and taste." She also corresponded with Frederic Ward Putnam, curator of Harvard's Peabody Museum, who wanted to borrow some of the items she had collected from the Kansas Indian tribes for display.[9]

In between writing letters and entertaining visitors, Owen was hard at work on her first novel, *The Daughter of Alouette*. Leland apparently assisted in finding a publisher for the book, and in November 1895, Owen signed a contract with Methuen and Company, a recently established British publisher that would also publish books by Rudyard Kipling, Oscar Wilde, and Robert Lewis Stevenson. Methuen published *The Daughter of Alouette* in May 1896.

In some respects, the protagonist of *The Daughter of Alouette* is reminiscent of the character of Tarias in Owen's 1889 story "The Taming of Tarias." Taminnika is the Métis child of a French trader named Pierre Rulo and a Pawnee mother called Tite Alouette. After the death of her mother, the infant Taminnika is taken in by Elias Zone, a European American Methodist minister, and his wife Alice in Robidoux Town, a thinly disguised version of St. Joseph. Though she lives a happy childhood with her adopted parents, their daughter Lily, and their two slaves, Uncle Washington and Aunt Nancy, Taminnika troubles the family with her inability to suppress a tendency toward behavior the Zones considered to be wild and un-ladylike. This penchant for unruliness ultimately leads the Zones to send her to a finishing school in Louisville, Kentucky.

Despite Taminnika's best efforts to live in the white world, after her return from school a series of encounters draws her toward her American Indian roots. At a gala party held at the home of a well-to-do local family, a visiting St. Louis socialite publically embarrasses Taminnika by inquiring loudly to those around her if she "was the pretty half-breed there has been so much joking about."[10]

When word of the incident spreads through Robidoux Town, a local African American hoodoo conjurer, Queen Ahola, tries to en-tice Taminnika into becoming her protégée. During a late-night meeting, Ahola questions the young woman's loyalty to the whites who raised her. "Could it be pleasant, do you think, for [your In-dian ancestors] to return to earth, and find you copying the life of the enemies who drove them to their death," the conjurer inquires. We learn that Ahola, who is three-quarters white, despises whites because they judge her by her one-quarter African American an-cestry and will not accept her as one of their own. She attempts to persuade Taminnika to share this disdain. "We are the children that should never have been born," she tells Taminnika. "We are the mixed bloods that, while despising our mothers, pity them; and hate their fathers the more on their account."[11]

Though Taminnika rejects the queen's dark invitation, her resolve to live in white society is further tested when she meets the noble young Ioway leader Chief Mohosca.[12] Owen endows this novel's leading American Indian character with the stoic strength and solid virtue that are traits of the stereotype known as the Noble Savage. Throughout the novel, Mohosca plays the role of cultural outsider who appears aloof and morally superior in his interactions with the whites. In one dramatic incident, Mohosca is falsely accused of stealing a white man's horse. As lawmen scuffle with Mohosca in an attempt to arrest him for the crime, Taminnika manages to take away the sheriff's revolver and passes it to Mohosca. In a display of his nobility, the Ioway leader politely and indifferently returns the gun to its owner without attempting to use it. Though Mohosca is ultimately exonerated in the theft, the incident renders him perma-nently smitten with Taminnika. Much to Reverend Zone's horror, the young Ioway spends many long nights outside the family home, attempting to court the object of his affection with music that he plays on a wooden flute.

Taminnika's initial resistance to Mohosca's overtures weakens when a distant Pawnee cousin asks for her help in performing a mourning ritual back on the reservation. As Taminnika considers the call to return to her mother's people, she is amazed that "there awakened in [her] breast . . . a fierce yearning to go to the sad old relative." She also recognizes that this event will change her life. "'I shall be sure where my place is ever after. If I make the visit,' she tells herself."[13]

In fact, Taminnika does find her place during her stay on the reservation. She attends the annual Green Corn dance where, despite her strict Methodist upbringing, Taminnika is unable to resist being drawn into the circle of dancers where she clasps hands with Mohosca "as if it were the ceremonial of the married ones." The experience leads to an epiphany for Taminnika, who sobs, "O Spirit of my mother's race, I hear you call . . . I come! Thy people shall be my people."[14]

While Taminnika struggles with her sense of ethnicity, the noble chief Mohosca is likewise forced to confront his own identity. When Taminnika's father, Reverend Zone, declares that he will not give his adopted daughter away to someone who is not a Christian, Mohosca realizes that in order to win her, he must court her in the manner of the whites. He therefore dons European American clothing and allows himself to be "cribbed, cabined and confined" in a linen suit and leather boots so that he is properly dressed to walk Taminnika and her parents home from church.

Despite his efforts to conform to the white world, it is Mohosca's "savage" strength that ultimately wins Taminnika's heart.[15] His opportunity comes one evening after a would-be white suitor kidnaps Taminnika while she is standing outside the church. While Reverend Zone and his male parishioners dither about the best way to pursue the kidnappers, Mohosca strips off his "cramping boots" and "hampering coat" and runs like "never even an Iowa[y] ran before" in an effort to rescue Taminnika. Muddy roads slow the progress of the kidnappers' horses and allow Mohosca to catch them on foot. Drawing his war club "from the pocket his tailor had destined

for more pacific instruments," the stealthy warrior disables the cap-
tors and rescues Taminnika. Weeks later the two are married and
return to the reservation to live among the Ioway.[16]

Like "The Taming of Tarias," *The Daughter of Alouette* is noteworthy in that it portrays a world in which people from various ethnic and cultural backgrounds live and work near one another. As
a result, Owen's Robidoux Town is a place where ethnic identities
are often mixed and ambiguous. Several of her characters, such as
Taminnika and the voodoo priestess Queen Ahola, are from mixed
ethnic backgrounds. Yet while Owen acknowledges the complexity
of ethnic heritage, she portrays racial identity as being simple and
static, especially for American Indians. While Taminnika valiantly
attempts to fit into the white world, she is ultimately drawn "back
to the blanket" and to life with Mohosca on the reservation. Film
historian Joanna Hearne has noted that Taminnika's struggle was
a popular one that found its way into many novels and films in the
early twentieth century. American Indian characters that had received a European American education and had lived in the Anglo
world were often pulled back to their tribes. According to Hearne,
this depicted a popular myth based on the perception that educated
and mixed-blood Indian people who lived in white communities
possessed an inherent "call of the wild" that would draw them back
to the villages of their ancestors.

Owen's tale of Taminnika and Mohohsca relies heavily on the
popular myth of the Noble Savage. This concept is usually associated with the eighteenth-century philosopher Jean Jacques Rousseau. Rousseau's use of the concept has generally been interpreted
as an illustration of his Romantic ideal of a natural state of man who
was neither stuck in the ignorant state of complete wildness nor corrupted by the burden of life of complete civilization. Because Rousseau's Noble Savage existed somewhere in between these worlds,
he embodied both the nobility of virtue and the innocence of living
in harmony with nature. Ter Ellingson has shown, however, that
Rousseau stated clearly that this version of the Noble Savage was a
"deliberate work of fiction" and that he used it to critique so-called
civilized life, not to promote an ideal state of human existence.[17]

As it turns out, Rousseau did not invent the concept of the Noble
Savage. Ellingson has traced the idea's first appearance back more
than a century before Rousseau's birth, to the French lawyer and

ethnographer Marc Lescarbot's 1609 *Histoire de la Nouvelle France* (*History of New France*). During his visit to the New World in 1606 and 1607, Lescarbot had been astonished to observe that the Indian population lived successfully in a society that did not appear to include a legal system. Based partly on his own observations and on the accounts of others who had traveled to New France, Lescarbot's book addressed this point by introducing the Noble Savage as a legal construct that attempted, as Ellingson put it, to "account for the problem of societies that could exist in the absence of anything Europeans might recognize as legal codes or institutions, by projecting a model drawn from European nobility that could satisfactorily account for the absence of a wide range of European-style political and legal constructs."[18] In other words, Lescarbot believed American Indians could thrive without the apparent rule of civil law because they were guided by a parallel code of conduct based on their inherent virtue.

On the North American continent, the ideal of the Noble Savage fit with European immigrants' views of American Indians. As early as 1694, Père Chauchetière, a Jesuit missionary living among the Huron, reported, "We see in the savages the fine remains of human nature which are entirely corrupted among civilized people. Indeed, all . . . who have lived among the savages reckon that life is passed more sweetly among them than among us."[19]

The Noble Savage became such an established fixture in European writings about the New World that it remained popular in works of fiction and art and in travel and anthropological writings well into the twentieth century. While Chauchetière's Noble Savage seemed carefree and bucolic, cultural historian Brian Dippie notes that by the nineteenth century this literary and artistic convention appeared "as a variation on the brooding, ill-starred creature of Romantic thought."[20] Silent, strong, uncomplicated, and untroubled by the trappings of contemporary culture, the Noble Savage was an exotic antidote to the worries and difficulties of civilized life.

On the one hand, Owen uses the myth of the Noble Savage to add a romantic element to what is essentially a love story. Young Mohosca is strong, quiet, handsome, and athletic, yet his heart is true and his character is uncontaminated by the greed and vice that have tainted many of his European American neighbors. He is a warrior who refuses to raise a hand to defend himself from a sheriff's posse but will fight to rescue the woman he loves. His nobility is his strength, yet it also makes him vulnerable to Taminnika's charms.

On the other hand, Owen also employs the Noble Savage stereotype in order to tell us that even though native people occupied Missouri's western border in the 1840s and 1850s, they had no place in the European American culture that was developing there. Mohosca is an outsider whose manners, culture, and lifestyle ensure that he will never find a comfortable place in white society. While he attempts to assimilate by wearing a linen suit and leather boots, he is unable to overcome his Indian identity and ultimately sheds his clothing to save Taminnika from her white kidnappers. When Mohosca marries Taminnika, the newlyweds follow their native hearts and choose to live with the Ioway on their reservation outside of "civilized" Missouri. Throughout the story, Owen wants us to believe that this ending is inevitable because neither of her native characters is able to fully assimilate to life in the refined world of the whites.

Owen was disappointed with *The Daughter of Alouette*, so much so that she did not send a copy of the novel to Charles Leland until two years after its publication. "I am afraid you will not like it," she wrote after finally asking the publisher to forward a copy to her mentor in 1898. "I was in a great glow about it when it was just finished, but in print it was not the same thing to me."[21] Leland must have had kind words for the book, however, because Owen thanked him for his compliments on it in a later letter.

Owen's second book was not as widely reviewed as her first book, *Old Rabbit*, had been. Nonetheless, William Wells Newell reviewed *The Daughter of Alouette* in the *Journal of American Folklore*. In his review, Newell treated the book as a work of folklore written in the form of fiction. He called attention to Owen's richly detailed descriptions of Potawatomi rituals of mourning and courtship, and he quoted extensively from a scene in which Owen described a procession of Indians who had just broken camp. However, Newell conspicuously stopped short of offering his opinion as to whether he felt the book was successful as either a work of fiction or a work of folklore.[22]

After the publication of *The Daughter of Alouette*, Owen briefly shifted her attention away from American Indians in order to undertake a project that focused on Gypsies. The term *Gypsy* has been used in reference to various nomadic ethnic groups that originate in Eastern Europe, Central Asia, and the Middle East. The largest ethnic group to be commonly referred to as Gypsies is the Romani people from Central and Eastern Europe. During Owen's lifetime, Romani immigrants lived in camps throughout the United States. Charles Leland, who published two books about Romanis and their magic, may have inspired Owen's interest in them. The study of Romani culture was especially popular in Europe, and Leland was a member of a Gypsy-Lore Society in Budapest, Hungary. Owen also attended a lecture on Romani folklore presented at the Chicago Folk-Lore Society by David Mae Ritchie in 1895. Regardless of how Owen was inspired to focus on Romani culture, it is not difficult believe that it was their reputation for picturesque clothing, magical spells, and music that drew her to them.[23]

By 1898, Owen was at work on a novel she called *An Ozark Gypsy* about a girl who was half white and half Romani. The work may have been inspired, in part, by Mary Palmer, a Romani woman whom Owen called the most accomplished liar and cheat she had ever met. The two met when Owen discovered Palmer camped on her property with two children, dogs, and horses. Upon their meeting, Palmer asked Owen for a loan and told her how her cruel landlord was attempting to extort money from her. When Owen informed Palmer that she was the owner of the land on which the small family was camped, Palmer laughed and said, "Well! You've got a joke on me this time."[24]

While working on *An Ozark Gypsy*, Owen also expressed an interest in astrology, palmistry, and the occult. She described for Leland two friends who were professional astrologers. "Their waiting room is like the kingdom of Heaven, filled with 'all sorts and conditions of men'—and women," from housemaids to the "bediamonded contingent" of wealthy citizens. She informed Leland that she had become friends with the astrologers because she knew more about the occult than they. She also mentioned that a medium named Slade was to hold a séance at her home. "If I find out 'how he does it,'" she wrote to Leland, "I'll let you know."[25]

By December 1898, Owen had completed the manuscript for *An Ozark Gypsy* and sent it to T. Fisher Unwin, her publisher in London. By March 1899, however, she had received no word from Unwin regarding plans for publishing the novel.[26] While it appears that the novel was eventually published—it is listed in several bibliographies of Owen's publications—researchers have not been able to locate a copy of the book.

While Owen seems to have been very active professionally at the turn of the twentieth century, the period was a difficult one for her on a personal level. An influenza epidemic nearly killed her already-ailing mother in September 1898. Earlier in the year, Owen had been called to make an emergency trip to Pittsburg, Pennsylvania, where her nephew, the son of her sister Florence Owen Orr, lingered with a life-threatening fever for three months. As his health finally began to improve, Florence's husband William became ill with a liver ailment. In a letter to Leland, Owen reported that the trip had taken an emotional toll on her and that her work had been neglected for several months.[27]

Though Owen shared the responsibility of caring for family members with her sisters Luella and Juliette, scheduling became difficult

Mary Alicia Owen, c. 1900.
(Courtesy of the Missouri State
Archives)

as both Mary and Luella began to travel more frequently for professional reasons. Luella Owen had begun to explore caves in the early 1890s. By the middle of the decade, she was traveling throughout the Ozarks and to the Black Hills of South Dakota as she prepared the manuscript for her book *Cave Regions of the Ozarks and Black Hills*. After the book was published in 1898, Luella spent much of her time closer to home researching the loess hills that run parallel to the Missouri River from Kansas City north to Sioux City, Iowa. This work was interrupted in 1900, however, by a yearlong world tour that she undertook as member of the American Geological Society.[28]

A voracious reader of newspapers, Mary Owen also occasionally allowed world events to distract her from her work. In the summer of 1898, for example, she sent Leland several letters in which she expressed her exasperation over the Spanish-American War. In one particularly passionate letter, Owen ranted not only against the Spanish but the French, the Germans, and all European aristocrats. "I can't be 'calm and dignified' just yet," she wrote in closing, adding that if the Atlantic squadron performed their duty successfully, her next letter might be more subdued.[29] For the next three months, she kept Leland updated on the latest war news by sending him letters and clippings. In August, she described for him the celebration that she could see from the veranda of her house when peace was declared.

As she worked to balance her professional career with her personal life, Owen, who turned fifty in 1900, began to endure physical setbacks of her own. In 1898 and 1899 she complained to Leland of suffering from malaria. Malaria, which is an infectious disease that is transferred to people from mosquitoes, had long been a problem in river communities, which tended to have an abundance of swampy, low-lying land. Owen told Leland that the disease had slowed her progress in writing *An Ozark Gypsy*.[30] Her writing was further hindered by rheumatism, from which she suffered severely by 1902. "There is no doubt about it. I am an old woman," Owen wrote to Leland in June of that year. "Gray hairs did not convince me, nor increasing weight warn me that the dignity of age was about all that time had left me, but when rheumatism took me by my right hand and wrung it with intimate grip of a companion who had come to stay, I succumbed—nay more, I groveled."[31]

Luella Agnes Owen, c. 1900. One of the three renowned Owen sisters, Ella, as her family called her, made a name for herself as a geologist. She wrote about the caves in the Ozarks and South Dakota and the loess hills of the Missouri River valley. (Courtesy of the Missouri State Archives)

However, middle age, weight, malaria, and rheumatism failed to keep Mary at home for long. In the same letter in which she complained to Leland about being "old," she wrote, "I must go over to the Indian Country as soon as my hand recalls its cunning well enough for me to 'do' my hair and button my jacket." During the first years of the twentieth century Owen was once again absorbed in American Indian culture. As the new century began, she focused her attention on the Sac and Fox of Kansas, and on their relatives the Sac and Fox in Oklahoma and the Meskwaki in Iowa, with the intention of publishing a book about them.

Seven

Vanishing Indians, 1900–1904

The Sac, or Sauk (Thakiwa), also known as the People of the Yellow Earth, and the Fox (Meskwaki), or People of the Red Earth, are two individual nations so closely affiliated with one another that by the 1700s many outsiders considered them to be one tribe. Part of the Algonquin language group, the Sac and Fox migrated from the East Coast before European contact, and they first encountered the French in the region of the Great Lakes in the seventeenth century. Wars with the French and the Iroquois pushed them into northeast Missouri and northern Illinois where they lived until 1804. That year William Henry Harrison, a general who would one day become president of the United States, persuaded four low-level Sac and Fox headmen to sign a treaty with the U.S. government in which they ceded land on both sides of the Mississippi stretching from St. Louis north into present-day Wisconsin. The Sac and Fox leader Black Hawk was enraged over the treaty and openly contested its validity for decades.[1]

During the War of 1812, the tribe divided into bands that the U.S. government labeled the Sac and Fox of the Mississippi and the Sac and Fox of the Missouri. The Mississippi branch of the tribe remained near the contested land ceded in the 1804 treaty. Armed by British traders operating from the region around Green Bay, in present-day Wisconsin, this band joined pro-British members of the Ioway and engaged in skirmishes against the United States. In an effort to pull the Ioway and the Sac and Fox away from the conflict, Superintendent of Indian Affairs William Clark succeeded in persuading pro-American members of each tribe to settle farther west near a trading post he established around the present-day town of Glasgow, Missouri. This branch of the tribe became known as the Sac and Fox of the Missouri and eventually settled even farther west, near the future site of Joseph Robidoux's trading post. By the late 1820s, the Sac and Fox of the Missouri were assigned to live near the U.S. government's Ioway subagency, which was located on the Platte River near the present-day town of Agency, Missouri, in Buchanan County.

About that time, the Sac and Fox of the Mississippi were living in the eastern section of present-day Iowa. In 1828, the Sac and Fox headman Black Hawk decided to return to the east side of the Mississippi River to reclaim the land that his people had lost in the treaty of 1804. Black Hawk's act of resistance resulted in an immediate military buildup of 1,800 American militiamen in the Mississippi River valley and eventually, in 1832, led to an armed conflict known as the Black Hawk War.[2] Though short-lived, the so-called war spread the fear of an Indian rebellion throughout American settlements in the Mississippi and Missouri River valleys. Eager to reassure settlers, the military pursued Black Hawk and his impoverished people, who by the summer of 1832 had decided to return to the west side of the Mississippi River. On August 2, 1832, Black Hawk tried to surrender to Captain Throckmorton aboard an American steamboat, the *Warrior*. Mistaking the surrender for an attack, riflemen aboard the boat killed dozens of Sac and Fox people as they tried to cross the Mississippi River while pro-American members of the Sioux nation killed dozens more who had safely made it to the Iowa side. In all, as many as 300 Sac and Fox people died in what is now known as the Bad Axe Massacre. While Black Hawk survived the massacre, he surrendered to General Henry Atkinson at Prairie du Chien soon afterward.[3]

The notoriety that Black Hawk gained as an "outlaw" before his surrender earned him the status of a celebrity in American popular culture. After spending the winter of 1832–1833 as a prisoner of the U.S. military in Jefferson Barracks near St. Louis, the Sac and Fox leader, accompanied by a military escort, embarked on a tour of the eastern United States. In the Ohio River towns of Cincinnati and Wheeling, hundreds of people turned out to catch a glimpse of the famous war chief as he sailed past aboard a steamboat. In Washington, Baltimore, Philadelphia, and New York, Black Hawk was treated to parties, sightseeing tours, and meetings with important government officials, including President Andrew Jackson. In 1834, he published his famous *Life of Black Hawk*. In his autobiography, which he had dictated to Antoine Leclair, an interpreter at the Sac and Fox Agency, the aging headman had the chance to tell his version of the events of his life and of the Black Hawk War. Black Hawk died in 1837 near the agency in what is now Van Buren County, Iowa. Violence followed him even in death. Thieves, hoping to cash in on the warrior's fame, stole Black Hawk's body and displayed his bones in a museum in Burlington, Iowa, where they were eventually destroyed in a fire.[4]

As the state of Iowa prepared to enter the Union in the 1840s, the government again moved the Sac and Fox of the Mississippi, this time to a reservation in the southeastern section of present-day Kansas. In 1857, some Meskwakis returned to Iowa where they bought 80 acres of land along the Iowa River near the town of Tama. There, they have been able to maintain their language and many of their cultural traditions to this day. The Sac and Fox people who stayed in the Kansas Territory moved in 1869 to a new reservation in the Indian Territory, now known as the state of Oklahoma, where they eventually became known as the Sac and Fox Nation of Oklahoma.[5]

Meanwhile, the Sac and Fox of the Missouri had also moved to a new home west of the Missouri River. In September 1836, leaders of the Missouri branch and the Ioway joined their agent Andrew Hughes at Fort Leavenworth to sign a treaty that became known as the Platte Purchase agreement. In the agreement, the Ioway, Sac and Fox, Otoe-Missouria, Omaha, Yankton Sioux, and Santee Sioux ceded to the United States all of their rights and claims to the land between the state of Missouri's western border and the Missouri River. A short time later, the state of Missouri annexed the land. For their claims, the Ioway and the Sac and Fox were given $7,500 and received two separate land reserves of 200 square miles on the south bank of the Grand Nemaha River near the border between present-day Kansas and Nebraska. On the reservation, the Sac and Fox of the Missouri adopted a European American agricultural lifestyle and became the most acculturated of the tribe's three branches. This branch of the tribe lived closest to St. Joseph, and it was the one with which Mary Owen had the most contact.[6]

Owen's relationship with the Sac and Fox was complex because, while she empathized with them, she also seems to have viewed them as a resource that she could mine for artifacts and information. While she felt a certain kinship with American Indian people, she did not see them as equal collaborators in her fieldwork. Her interactions with them were driven by her desire to gather information about their lifestyle, religion, and ceremonies. She viewed the Indians with whom she worked as cultural informants and treated them in much the same way that she might have treated the cooks, maids, and gardeners she hired to work in her home.

We have already seen how Owen asserted herself over King Alexander and the other conjurers with whom she consulted while working on *Old Rabbit* and on her unfinished second book on hoodoo. Consider, for instance, the scene in *Old Rabbit* in which she admonished King Alexander to speak more clearly so she could accurately record the words he said while he made Charles Leland's luck ball.[7] Owen's position of authority was even more clearly defined in those instances when she paid her informants. We do not know if Owen regularly paid for information, but we do know that on at least one occasion, she made it clear that payment was contingent on an informant's ability and willingness to provide her with the information she wanted. Such was the case when Owen visited Ellen Merida, the conjurer who lived in Plattsburg, Missouri. After Merida's neighbors interrupted their visit, she refused to talk about hoodoo. When Owen threatened not to pay Merida unless she received the information she wanted, the conjurer led Owen to another room and quietly asked her to return another time.[8]

Evidence suggests that when Owen was unable to buy the information she wanted, she was not above taking it. Such was the case when she acquired the black conjuring stone that became one of Charles Leland's prized possessions. Though the manner in which she acquired the stone would be deemed highly unethical and illegal today, Owen felt justified in her actions because she believed the previous owner of the stone to be unworthy, dissipated, and malicious.[9]

This behavior portrays Owen as a collector who was not always interested in a reciprocal relationship with her informants. Such willingness to exploit her informants suggests that she placed her own work and desires above the respect she had for the people and the cultures with whom she worked. Anthropologist Renato Rosaldo has referred to those who practiced this authoritative manner of gathering cultural information as "lone ethnographers." As a lone ethnographer, Owen operated as a culture collector rather than cultural participant. According to Rosaldo, lone ethnographers operated under the assumption that their informants had no agency in the transaction of information gathering. Lone ethnographers believed it was the informant's role to provide raw material in the form of speech or artifacts that the lone ethnographer could record, process, and distribute, often in the form of museum exhibits or books and articles. Rosaldo argues that this unequal type of intercultural relationship, which was not uncommon in Owen's time, is a form of colonialism that rendered collectors "complicit with the imperialist domination" that marked the era in which Owen worked.[10]

But even lone ethnographers did not always get all of the information they desired. Owen knew that tribal members often placed limits on the amount of information they were willing to share with her. While she was allowed to attend dances, Owen was most likely excluded from private ceremonies. While she blamed her exclusion, in part, on the missionaries and Indian agents, her access to information was also shaped by the likelihood that because she was a woman, tribal cultural norms dictated that she spend most of her time among the Sac and Fox working with other women. Ever curious, she occupied herself by observing the daily activities and listening to the stories of her female acquaintances, and quizzing them for any nuggets of additional knowledge she could gain.[11]

One of Owen's informants was Mary Lasley, who was also known as Bee-wah-thee-wah, or Singing Bird. Lasley's father was said to have been Black Hawk and her mother the granddaughter of an Ioway leader named Standing Bear. In the summer of 1902, Owen was writing catalogue descriptions of nearly a hundred Sac and Fox items she had collected and donated to the English Folk-Lore Society. The catalogue would be published as part of her 1904 book, *Folk-lore of the Musquakie Indians*. Lasley provided Owen with information about some of the artifacts she bought from tribal members. She also provided Owen with cultural information and with traditional stories. On one occasion, after Owen bought a catlinite cup that the seller claimed had belonged to Black Hawk's rival Keokuk, she took it to Lasley to confirm its authenticity.

Owen reported that Lasley told her she "had no good heart" for her father because he was not a "gentleman." Lasley reportedly told Owen this was because while he claimed to have had one wife, he actually had eight—one of whom had been her Ioway mother. Furthermore, as a war chief, Black Hawk had come from a family that Lasley believed was less prestigious than that in which her mother was raised. While it is not clear that any of Lasley's information was accurate, Owen valued her as an informant and the two collaborated on the publication of a collection of traditional stories and information about cultural rituals that appeared under Lasley's name in *Journal of American Folklore* in 1902.[12]

One Sac and Fox man did play an important role in Owen's quest for knowledge about the tribe. Owen identified Nekon-Mackintosh, also known as John Mackintosh, as the Sac's and Fox's "head shaman." After the death of his parents, Mackintosh was, according to Owen, raised by the family of an Anglo-American physician. He studied medicine and contemplated taking over his adopted father's practice. Instead, the young man returned to the Sac and Fox where he sought to learn the secrets of traditional healers and use his mixture of native and nonnative knowledge for the benefit of his people.[13]

Despite the assistance of these and other unnamed informants, Owen still found that on a number of occasions she was unable to find out the significance of certain details of Sac and Fox culture. Though Owen was not averse to questioning her informants, she wrote that they remained silent on some topics, even when she repeated the same question several times. At other times, her subjects provided answers that she found frustratingly evasive. Once, while observing a Green Corn dance, the Sac and Fox precursor to the powwow, she asked a girl why participants marked their faces with white paint. The girl simply replied that it was "fun."[14]

Owen was particularly vexed at her inability to get at what she perceived as the essence of Sac and Fox culture: something she called "Mee-sham." According to Owen, the Mee-sham was a covenant or a "mysterious something" that had been passed down from the tribe's ancestors. She reported that all Sac and Fox men knew what the Mee-sham was, but that they had never revealed it to the women. When Owen asked her female informants what they thought it might be, some speculated that it was the hide of a black wolf, a bag filled with potent medicine, or a roll of painted skins. On another occasion, when she pressed a Sac and Fox man on the essence of Mee-sham, she reported that he answered cryptically, "What for you ask? Him all same like your Ark and Covenant."[15]

In assessing Owen's study of Sac and Fox culture, the literary critic Neil Schmitz has viewed Mee-sham as a metaphor for the cultural information that Anglo-American folklorists and ethnographers like Mary Alicia Owen could never attain because of their status as outsiders. He labeled this phenomenon the "Mee-sham effect." Mee-sham, writes Schmitz, represents that which "is averted from Euro-American knowledge, [and] will never be captured." Viewed this way, the Mee-sham effect acknowledges that Sac and Fox people did in fact exercise agency in their relationship with Owen. While she initiated the exchange of stories and artifacts with her Sac and Fox acquaintances, they ultimately controlled the process of exchange by determining what they were willing to reveal to and share with her.[16]

Another facet of the Mee-sham effect exhibited itself in Owen's apparent inability to fully appreciate and comprehend some of the cultural information tribal members did share with her. Sandra Massey, an author and cultural preservation representative of the Sac and Fox Nation of Oklahoma, has expressed concern about inaccuracies in Owen's work. Massey believes that, as an outsider, Owen would not have been allowed to participate in most tribal ceremonies. She believes that Owen sometimes compensated for her lack of firsthand knowledge by presenting conjecture about these events as fact.[17]

Ioway-Otoe-Missouria linguist and scholar Jimm GoodTracks has pointed out one instance in which Owen's lack of knowledge about Sac and Fox language and culture led her to make erroneous assumptions about stories she collected from Mary Lasley. Published as "Sac and Fox Tales" in the *Journal of American Folklore* in 1902, at least some of these stories were not from the Sac and Fox at all. The story "Possum" was published in English with a phonetic version of what Owen apparently believed to be the Algonquin-based language spoken by the Sac and Fox. After analyzing the phonetics, Good-Tracks determined that the story was in fact written in the Báxoje, a

Siouan language spoken by the Ioway and Otoe-Missouria people. This "Sac and Fox tale" was actually an Ioway story. GoodTracks determined that the other stories and cultural information in the article were Ioway. Lasley had likely learned the stories from Ioway relatives on her mother's side of the family.[18]

Owen was not the only Anglo-American traveling to Sac and Fox settlements for the purpose of study and research in the late nineteenth and early twentieth centuries. A Unitarian minister and anthropology lecturer at the University of Iowa named Duren J. H. Ward spent two months at the Meskwaki settlement near Tama, Iowa, in the summer of 1905. Supported by the State Historical Society of Iowa, Ward's research trip is noteworthy because he made audio recordings of several oral histories and photographed many of his Meskwaki informants.[19]

While Owen's time with the tribe was spent primarily in the company of women, Ward seems to have spent most of his visit with men. As a result, his observations and writing on the Meskwakis focus primarily on tribal politics and the tribe's relations with the U.S. government. Owen, for example, wrote that the Meskwakis' return to Iowa in the 1850s was a "revolt of the squaws." Owen's female informants had told her that a measles epidemic had killed many small children in the spring of 1831. These children were buried in Iowa, and their mothers could not bear being separated from them when they moved to Kansas in 1847. "The mother who dies far from her baby's grave loses her darling forever," Owen wrote in *Folk-lore of the Musquakie Indians*, but "the mother who keeps near it has two chances for happiness." According to Owen, the bereaved mothers informed their husbands that they intended to return to Iowa to be with their children and that the men could follow or stay behind. "They set out," Owen wrote, "and the men followed and overtook them." [20]

In contrast, Duren Ward chronicled the Meskwakis' return to Iowa from the perspective of the tribal government and the Meskwaki men. Working from a history prepared by tribal secretary C. H. Chuck, also known as Cha-ka-ta-ko-si, and state land records, Ward cast the move as the outcome of a political decision reached by tribal leaders. Enhanced by the oral history interviews and a search of land records and legal statutes, Ward's version of the story involves

a history of the land purchases and the laws passed by Iowa's Fifth
General Assembly that permitted Meskwaki people to return to
the state. Ward and his informants meticulously collected a list of
all tribal land purchases and plotted them on a plat map, which he
published in the *Iowa Journal of History and Politics* in 1906. Another
of Ward's lasting legacies is the collection of photographic portraits
of Meskwaki people he commissioned from J. S. Moore, a studio
photographer from Toledo, Iowa. The photos, now in the collection
of the State Historical Society of Iowa, provide a document of men,
women, and children, often in their traditional clothing.[21] Ward's
published articles about the Meskwakis are notable for their avoid-
ance of religious and cultural matters. As an outsider like Owen,
Duren Ward more than likely also struggled with the Mee-sham effect. Perhaps to overcome this, he tended to focus on tribal politics,
history, and topics that he could verify in public records.

It is worth noting that while Owen and Ward were making their
investigations into Sac and Fox history and culture, at least one
tribe member was also collecting oral history and artifacts. William
Jones, also known as Mekasihawa or Black Eagle, was one of the
first American Indians to be formally trained as an anthropologist.
The son of Henry Clay Jones, whose mother was Sac and Fox, and
Sarah Penny, who was English, Jones was raised by his grandfather
Katiqua, a traditional member of the Sac and Fox Nation of Oklahoma. While living with his grandfather, Jones learned to speak the
Sac and Fox language fluently and participated in tribal ceremonies
and activities. At age eighteen, Jones had the opportunity to study
at the Hampton Normal and Agricultural Institute in Hampton, Virginia. He went on to attend Harvard where he met Frederic Ward
Putnam, an anthropologist who was the curator of the Peabody Museum. In 1897, Putnam sent Jones to collect traditional stories at the
Meskwaki settlement in Iowa. Four years later, Jones entered Columbia University to study with Franz Boas. Under Boas's direction,
he returned to the Sac and Fox settlements in 1901 and 1902 to collect more stories. In 1907, the Field Museum in Chicago employed
Jones to travel once more to the Meskwaki settlement in Iowa, this
time to collect artifacts. Jones published several articles about Sac
and Fox ethnology and folklore in his short career, including his
1907 "Fox Texts," which presented Algonquin oral literature in the

Sac and Fox language with English translations. William Jones was killed at the age of thirty-eight while on a Field Museum expedition in the Philippines in 1909.[22]

The legacy of Jones's work is decidedly mixed. It has long been considered valuable because it was the work of a person who grew up inside the culture of the Sac and Fox and offered a rare insider's analysis of tribal oral history and artifacts. To this day, anthropologists look to "Fox Texts" as an authentic source of Sac and Fox culture. Yet the Meskwaki writer Sophilia Keahna characterizes Jones as being "a morally judgmental scientist who often employed harsh, manipulative means to acquire the crafts, artifacts, handiwork, and information." Meskwaki historian Johnathan Buffalo has suggested that simply because Jones was Sac and Fox does not mean that his understanding of the culture was more accurate than Owen's. Noting that Jones was from the Sac and Fox Nation of Oklahoma and had not grown up with the Meskwakis in Iowa, Buffalo states, "He may have been of lineal descent from this tribe and might even have been able to speak the language but he was missing something very crucial . . . He lacked the many years of time that it takes to develop a good command of complex language, a solid understanding of the many overt and subtle social skills needed to navigate within the tribe, and proper religious contexts."[23]

As anthropological researchers, Duren Ward and William Jones were quite different. While Jones appears to have assumed authority because of his status as a cultural insider, Ward seemed to accept his status as an outsider and conducted his research accordingly. Armed with some formal training in history and anthropology, Ward focused on methodically documenting his research during his visit. Mary Owen, however, occupied a different position from both Ward and Jones. As a familiar figure in Sac and Fox settlements for at least two decades and as an adopted member of the tribe, Owen may have assumed that she had achieved some degree of status as a tribal insider and confidant. Even so, Owen was sometimes frustrated in her attempts to acquire information and artifacts. Obstacles such as the efforts of Indian agents and missionaries to suppress ceremonies and traditional gatherings, the evasiveness of some Sac and Fox informants, and the fact that she was ultimately an outsider prevented Mary Alicia Owen from gathering as much knowledge and information as she desired.[24]

Owen wrote to Charles Leland to express her frustration over her inability to collect information from her Sac and Fox informants. "I have collected a number of songs of mourning from the Sacs, but no history songs. I'll get the latter in time. I think I'm naturally an impatient person, and the Fates try me by having me wait, wait, wait for everything." On another occasion, she wrote to Leland, "It seems to me, sometimes, that nobody else in the whole world has to wait and wait for things as I do. One advantage I have, I finally do get what I am after."[25]

Leland's letters to Owen indicate that he believed her impatience was justified. "Go at [your collecting] earnestly, be among the first," he wrote to his protégée. "For I foresee that sooner or later, every scrap, good or bad, will be studied and admired . . . and men will wonder that among all the scholars of our age so few cared for such a marvelous record of the vanishing race. . . . Don't lose time."[26]

Leland advised Owen to conduct her research quickly for two reasons. Firstly, he believed she was working in a field that was not yet saturated with folklorists and ethnographers and she was gathering information no one had previously collected. His advice to her indicates that he wanted Owen to stake out her professional territory before other folklorists moved in and the field became crowded. Secondly, Leland felt that haste was necessary because, like many people of his time, he believed that American Indian people were quickly vanishing and that once they were gone, their oral traditions, ceremonies, and religious beliefs would vanish with them. In fact, many folklorists of the era believed they were in a race against time to salvage as much as they could before Indians vanished forever.

The effort to collect as much information as possible about the vanishing race of Indians extended to the intense scrutiny of pre-historic human remains found throughout North America. While Owen was conducting her research on the Sac and Fox, she and her sister Luella Owen took great interest in a skeleton discovered not far from St. Joseph. In February 1902, a famer named Martin Concannon discovered the skeleton of an adult female while digging a fruit cellar near the town of Lansing, Kansas. At the time, some believed "the Lansing Man" may have been 25,000 years old, which would have made it among the oldest ever to be found on the continent. "They had no idea of the value of their find," Owen wrote to Leland.

"Fortunately, a Kansas City professor and newspaper man went to investigate and called the attention of geologists and archaeologists everywhere. Kansas City got the skull and a Kansas museum got the greater part of the other bones—all, in fact, accept an arm bone that old Mr. Cincannon gave [Luella]. He said that as she was the first live lady to pay her respects to the ice lady, a *souvenir* was due her." Almost immediately, however, anthropologist Ales Hrdlicka questioned the authenticity of the Lansing Man by pointing out that the skull was nearly identical to those of nineteenth-century Indians. Hrdlicka argued that it was unlikely that such a modern skull was 25,000 years old. [27]

The idea of the Vanishing Indian was partially based on fact and partially on myth. The nineteenth century had seen a series of epidemics, forced removals, and so-called Indian Wars that had dramatically decreased Indian populations throughout the nation. Those Indian people who had survived had become wards of the U.S. government and had been forcibly confined to reservations. It was a fact that Indians were no longer the visible or cultural presence they had been a century earlier. The fact that Indian populations had dramatically decreased went hand in hand with a cultural myth that placed Indian people in the past. By the turn of the twentieth century, many Americans began to feel a sense of sympathy toward American Indians. This sympathy was mixed with a collective feeling of nostalgia Americans felt in the wake of the nation's rapid development. In the rush to fulfill their Manifest Destiny, Anglo-Americans had pushed Indian nations, buffalo, and the virgin wilderness to the edge of extinction.

The myth of the Vanishing Indian gained popularity as cities in the United States became increasingly industrialized and the lives of the urban Americans left them less connected to the natural world. Historians have noted that as North America evolved into a maze of towns, railroad tracks, and telegraph wires, European Americans began to nostalgically identify Indians with the passing wilderness. Literary critic Klaus Lubbers has noted, "Native Americans . . . were overwhelmingly associated with the past."[28] Many assumed that the new nation offered no place for American Indians and that they were doomed to disappear forever. As General John Benjamin Sanborn, a member of the post–Civil War Indian Peace Commission, lamented in the late 1860s, "Little can be hoped for [Indians] as a distinct people. The sun of their day is fast sinking in the western sky. It will soon go down in a night of oblivion that shall know no morning. . . . No spring time shall renew their fading glory, no future know their fame."[29]

Given the prevalence of the myth of the Vanishing Indian, it is no surprise that it became a major theme in Mary Alicia Owen's 1904 book *Folk-lore of the Musquakie Indians*. In his introduction to Owen's text, anthropologist E. Sidney Hartland lamented that Owen's study was especially valuable because the Sac and Fox "have been beaten; and they are now a dying people." Though they may carry on "in some measure, their ancient beliefs and institutions are passing away for ever."[30] With these words, Hartland defines the Sac and Fox as a culture that exists outside the parameter of European American civilization and that does not participate in its cultural and technical progress. Though they remained alive in the late nineteenth and early twentieth century, Hartland firmly associates the Sac and Fox with the ancient past.

In her own text, Owen supports Hartland's theme of the dying Sac and Fox by alluding to the many ways in which the link between their twentieth-century lives and their ancient history and beliefs is becoming increasingly precarious. For example, she describes the position of the tribal historian, the only person among the Sac and Fox who she believed had complete command of the oral history that documents the people's history. According to Owen, it was the historian's duty to recount the tribes' history in its entirety four times a year at government councils and anecdotally at dances and other ceremonies throughout the year. It was also his job to select a young boy with a good memory to serve as his student. Over the years, the historian helped the boy commit the oral literature of the Sac and Fox people to memory so that when the historian died, the history would be retained. Owen relates that this precarious method of transmitting the tribe's history had, on at least one occasion, nearly led to the history being lost altogether when the historian and his apprentice both died unexpectedly. "Then," Owen writes, "there was confusion and dismay" until a disabled boy "of low degree" revealed that he had often eavesdropped on the sessions during which the historian transmitted the nation's history to his student. So completely had the second boy memorized the lessons of the historian that "his grateful people broke rules for once . . . and set him on the council as historian."[31] By emphasizing the story of the nearly lost history, Owen seems to suggest that the Sac and Fox are unreliable stewards of their own history.

Owen further reinforces the theme of the vanishing traditions of the Sac and Fox in the catalogue portion of *Folk-lore of the Musquakie Indians*. In that section she cites the people's lost traditions as the reason for their shifting relationship with their material culture. She tells her readers that objects that were once utilitarian in nature, such as bows, arrows, war clubs, and pipes, are now used ceremonially in "historical drama[s] to illustrate what the tribal historian relates." To the "wild man surrounded by civilization and making a stand against it," she writes, "everything that relates to his free and savage past has become a ceremonial object."[32]

Even so, Owen portrayed tribal members as generally being uninterested or unable to care for their own material culture. She recounts stories of how this situation allowed her to buy several items. One person sold her a catlinite pipe because it had once been used by a "drunken chief" and was therefore tainted. Owen purchased a parfleche of painted buffalo hide "from a poor widow who had no sons to care for it," and a treaty belt that was sold by its owners "as a revenge for the affront of the Sacs on the Nemaha Reservation, who endeavored to have a few Musquakies on that reservation expelled." As Owen and other anthropologists and souvenir hunters sought to buy these exotic artifacts, many of the tribe's most culturally important relics slipped out of their possession. Of the four pipes used during meetings of the tribal council, for instance, Owen informs us that only one remained, and the secret of its whereabouts was, by her account, guarded as carefully as that of the Mee-sham.

In the past, some of these items might have been replaced or repaired by skilled craftspeople. Owen, however, expresses the opinion that many of the secrets of these craftspeople have also been lost. Sac and Fox women, she writes, no longer possess the ability to tan soft and supple hides, and few have the patience necessary to create the intricate beadwork that had been the hallmark of their ancestors. While it is impossible to know if Owen's assertion is accurate, it does show that she believed that the Sac and Fox were losing their ability to make and care for their traditional material culture.[33]

It is worth noting that in *Folk-lore of the Musquakie Indians*, Owen writes at length about just two Sac and Fox people. One is her informant Nikon-Mackintosh, the orphaned healer who had been raised by a European American doctor, whom she portrays as a variant of the Noble Savage. Owen's brief account of Mackintosh's life bears a similarity to that of Taminnika, the character she created in *The Daughter of Alouette*. Like Taminnika, Mackintosh returns to his people as an adult, but not with the intention of carrying "civilization to his people." The young doctor returns to assist the Sac and Fox by practicing "every art of ancient sorcery with such additions as his scientific knowledge may suggest." Owen infers that, despite his Anglo education and upbringing, Mackintosh, like Taminnika, has no place in the modern world because, as she says, "once an Indian, always an Indian."[34]

It is telling, perhaps, that Owen's most detailed account of a Sac and Fox individual in *Folk-lore of the Musquakie Indians* is devoted to No-chu-ning, who is literally a Vanishing Indian. When Owen introduces the young man, he is about to die of tuberculosis. In his last moments, No-Chu-ning's mother begs him to sing his death song. In traditional times, warriors who faced death in battle would sing of the good deeds they had accomplished in warfare and in life. But No-Chu-ning refused to sing a death song because, as Owen surmises, "no one raises his death song now." Owen asserts that this is because there is no point in wasting one's last breath to "tell of a few horse races won."[35] It is Owen's belief, in other words, that because the young man had accomplished little in life and had been felled by sickness rather than by a battlefield opponent, he had nothing of note to sing about.

Owen devotes ten pages to a detailed description of No-Chu-ning's death, burial, and the traditional ceremony performed to send off his spirit. After the man's body was wrapped, carried to a nearby hill and buried, the family observes a thirty-day period of mourning. At the end of that period, it was time for the man's ghost to be carried away. No-Chu-ning's family provided food for a feast, at which a place is set for the deceased man. As the feast draws to a close at sunset, a tribal leader announces that it was time for a designated ghost carrier to travel to a place that Owen referred to as the "Happy Hunting Ground." The ghost carrier, who serves as a surrogate for No-Chu-ning in the ceremony, mounts a horse and rides westward with an escort and with No-Chu-ning's spirit. Quietly returning home after dark, the ghost carrier assumes the role of the newly adopted son of No-Chu-ning's parents.[36]

This last ceremony seems to have had some potency for Owen. She had described a similar ceremony in *The Daughter of Alouette*. In that instance, Owen used the ritual as a literary device to draw Taminnika away from white civilization and back to the reservation. From her description of the ceremony in *The Folk-lore of the Musquakie Indians*, it is evident that Owen saw the carrying away of No-Chu-ning's spirit as a metaphor for the gloomy destiny of a race of people that she felt were doomed to vanish forever.

Writing in the British journal *Man*, a reviewer by the name of A. Hingston praised Owen for not only for collecting accounts of Musquakie ceremonies but for collecting the artifacts that go along with the ceremonies. He noted that while the catalogue portion of *Folklore of the Musquakie Indians* was "rarely poetic," the narrative section possessed a clarity that heightened its romantic quality. "The graphic simplicity of its descriptions transforms the reader into a sympathetic observer of the scene. . . . The 'Red Indian' has always been a favorite hero of poetry and romance. Miss Owen shows that the clear light of scientific observation increases, rather than dispels the glamour."[37]

Over the next few years, Owen would continue to write about the romantic myth of the Vanishing Indian, linking it to other Indian legends related to death and mourning. As we shall see, this resulted in the creation of a more powerful version of the myth that in many ways persists to this day.

Eight

"The Road to Paradise," 1905–1935

While she was still working on the manuscript for *The Folk-lore of the Musquakie Indians,* Mary Alicia Owen suffered the loss of her friend and mentor Charles Leland. Leland, who was living in Italy at the time of his death on March 20, 1903, had been in fragile health for some time and had suffered many physical and psychological setbacks in the last months of his life. In July 1902, Eliza Bella "Isabel" Fisher, his wife of nearly fifty years, had died. "I was so afraid that after the terrible strain you had given way completely," Owen wrote to Leland after learning of his wife's passing. "Heaven be praised that your patience and strength of will have brought you through the valley of the shadow and into the sunlight again with only a short illness."[1]

Owen continued to write to Leland after his wife's death with bits of local and family news, snippets of folklore that she had collected and nuggets of humor that seemed to be designed to cheer a grieving man. "I had two letters today," she wrote in July 1902. "One from the nuisance inspector telling me to cut down the sun flowers on a vacant lot I own, the other from a society requesting me to pledge myself to help preserve the wild flowers."[2]

"To read a letter like yours makes me realize how charming it would be to be able to talk to you," Leland replied in October 1902. "I am suffering more than I supposed it would be possible from the want of someone in my life to turn to, to consult, to talk with." Despite the fact that the two had met face-to-face on only a few occasions, Owen and Leland had grown very close during their fifteen-year correspondence. Leland was, without a doubt, the most important advisor in Owen's professional life. Without his guidance and support, it seems unlikely that Owen would have become a professional folklorist. Leland helped reassure and encourage Owen in her work, and he continued to do so during the last months of his life. "If I can help you in any way, I will with all my heart," he wrote to Owen less than five months before he died.[3]

At about the same time that Leland wrote those words of support to Owen, his apartment in Florence was burglarized. While he was upset about the loss of money and personal items, he was devastated by the fact that the thieves had stolen the black conjurer stone Owen had given him upon their first meeting in 1891. In February 1903, detectives somehow tracked the stolen stone to a woman whom they believed was using it to perform witchcraft. While Leland had the satisfaction of recovering the stone, his health continued to fail, and he died a month later at the age of seventy-nine.

Two days after his death, Owen wrote a letter of condolence to Leland's sister, Mrs. John Harrison, who had nursed him during his final days. "It is such a cruel loss, to the world at large as well as to those who had the bloom of his love and his friendship. He gave much from the treasures of his mind, but oh, there is so much that one so gifted cannot leave when he goes to a sphere of higher intelligence."[4]

The early years of the new century also brought other changes to the life of Mary Owen. While she had always drawn heavily on local sources for material that she used in her fiction and her folklore, Owen had, since the mid-1880s, focused on sharing her writing with national and international audiences, publishing in journals in England as well as the United States and traveling widely to conferences and meetings. Even before the publication of the *Folk-Lore of the Musquakie Indians*, however, Owen had begun to travel less frequently and seemed to return much of her professional attention to working on material that was written for audiences in the state of Missouri. There may have been a variety of reasons for this. In 1900, Mary's mother, Agnes Owen, celebrated her seventieth birthday. Agnes had been in poor health for the better part of two decades and was said to have been homebound for much of that time. Despite their busy professional schedules, Mary Owen and her sisters Luella and Juliette seem to have been devoted to their mother and spent much of their time engaged not only in her care, but in the day-to-day running of the household they shared. As her mother continued to decline, Mary Owen may have chosen to stay closer to St. Joseph so that she might share in as many of her mother's remaining days as possible.

Another reason that Owen may have chosen to remain closer to home is the likelihood that, as she aged, she found that it was more difficult to travel comfortably. Her chronic rheumatism, asthma, and malaria sometimes kept her at home for days or even weeks at a time. Age and excess weight seem to have made her more prone to illness and injury. In 1900, she described for Leland a knee injury she had suffered in a fall. Despite the injury, she traveled to St. Louis for a speaking engagement. "Not realizing that an injury to a joint was a very serious matter, I let it get very bad before I consulted a physician," she told her friend. The injury rendered her bedridden and unable to work for six weeks.[5]

But while the realities of aging may have persuaded Owen to travel less, her focus on local audiences may also have come from the fact that, after working more than two decades as a professional writer, she was becoming increasingly disenchanted with the politics of the publishing world. "I don't believe I'll ever amount to much as a writer," she wrote to Leland in 1899, "though I see in print in honorable places much worse writing than mine. New York and New England hold the balance of power, that is to say, their authors are sort of 'You-tickle-me-and-I'll-tickle-you' society, writing laudations for the members and disparaging or ignoring outsiders. Sectional prejudice isn't fair, but it's eminently human."[6]

It is not difficult to imagine that Owen took a certain amount of pleasure in her role as an outsider in the world of publishing. Though she occasionally admitted doubts about her work to Leland, Owen was a woman of deeply held opinions who could exhibit a strong air of self-confidence. Similarly, Owen sometimes took delight in defying convention or in voicing an unpopular point of view. Once, for example, when expressing to Leland her opinion that Ralph Waldo Emerson and Robert Browning were "obtuse" writers, she joked, "Of course, this is rank heresy and I deserve to be burnt, but burn I will rather than recant. My people have a trick of getting on the unpopular side and frying for it."[7] So it may have been with a strong sense of Show-Me State pride, rather than a pang of regret, that Owen began to distance herself from the Eastern publishing and academic establishment and focused an increasing amount of her attention on writing for and speaking to the people she felt she understood best, her fellow Missourians.

Owen regularly spoke about folklore to groups around Missouri. Some of her talks seem to have been designed to cultivate a community of interested people who would assist her in the preservation of Missouri folklore. In her effort to interest people in the topic, Owen found attentive audiences among various local and regional social organizations. As has already been noted, Owen had been active in a number of clubs since her teenage years. In the early years of the twentieth century, she was a member of the Wednesday Club and the Daughters of the American Revolution. She was also the fine arts chairperson of the City Federation of Women's Clubs, an organization made up of almost 500 women from seventeen St. Joseph organizations who came together to make the "city worth while."[8] Over the years, Owen spoke to many of these organizations on such topics as "The Study of Folk-Lore" and "Oracles and Witches." When she described these talks in letters to Leland, Owen never spoke condescendingly about her audiences. Instead, she revealed a desire to instruct her listeners on the topic of collecting folklore.

Owen's efforts to promote the cause of preserving Missouri's rich folklore led to her active participation in the Missouri Folk-Lore Society. Henry Marvin Belden, a professor of English at the University of Missouri, founded the society in 1906. Belden, who would become the president of the American Folklore Society in 1910 and 1911, was a collector of American and English folk ballads. A native of Connecticut and a graduate of Johns Hopkins University, he had arrived in Columbia, Missouri, in 1895. By 1903, he was an active member of the Writer's Club, which met in the office of the University of Missouri's English department for the purpose of collecting Missouri's folk songs and "literary material." By December 1906, the club had evolved into the Missouri Folk-Lore Society. Belden was the society's first secretary while Owen became its founding vice president. Two years later, the society's membership elected Owen as president, a position she held until the society became inactive in 1920.[9]

While Owen and Belden were never particularly close, their strong personalities and complimentary professional interests proved to benefit the society greatly in its early years. With his concentration in collecting folk songs, Belden fit squarely in the camp of literary folklorists. Left to his own devices, he would, no doubt, have steered the society in the same literary-minded direction that the Chicago Folk-Lore Society had followed in the 1890s. However, Owen was able to assert her influence to expand the scope of the Missouri Folk-Lore Society to include the study of "folklore in the broadest sense of the term, including customs, institutions, superstitions, signs, legends, language and literature of all races, so far as they are found in the state of Missouri."[10]

Under Belden's direction, the society published material that was intended to guide amateurs in the process of collecting Missouri folklore. To this effort, Owen contributed a short article called "Suggestions for Collectors of Negro and Indian Folk-Lore in Missouri." In the article, she passed on the advice of the British folklorist George Laurence Gomme, who warned, "The value of this work can only be measured by the amount of absolute precision and faithfulness with which each collector records every item of Folk-Lore." Owen told her readers that "superstitious beliefs and practices will cover almost the entire field" of folklore. She then listed twelve types of superstitions that collectors might be on the lookout for. These included superstitions about animals, witchcraft, medicine, magic, and fortunes. She closed her list by advising collectors that the best method of questioning informants was to ask them about their beliefs in an indirect fashion. Quoting William Shakespeare's character Polonius, she wrote, "By indirection, find direction out."[11]

Though age may have begun to force Owen to slow down a bit, it did little to extinguish her curiosity or her willingness to try new things. In 1909, as she neared the age of sixty, she published her first play, *The Sacred Council Hills*. In the play, Owen presented St. Joseph history and folklore in a form that was tailored specifically for a local audience. Jean Fahey Eberle maintains that Owen originally published *The Sacred Council Hills* in prose form in England in 1907. Unfortunately, no copies of that book are known to exist. Eberle asserts that Owen rewrote *The Sacred Council Hills* as a play, which she published herself, after someone requested that she create something for the students of St. Joseph High School to perform on stage.[12] Written for adolescents to perform in an era in which theatric melodramas were popular, the action and dialogue in *The*

Sacred Council Hills is highly stylized. The work is characterized by overwrought emotions, dramatic language, and Indian characters who sometimes deliver lines in rhyming couplet. In the play, as in *The Folk-Lore of the Musquakie Indians*, Owen again presents American Indians in a scenario that reinforces the popular notion that they are a vanishing race.

The play opens as several members of the Sac and Fox of the Missouri arrive in the Sacred Council Hills, the place on which present-day St. Joseph now stands. In the opening scene, Owen's Sac and Fox characters express gratitude to Manitou, the creator, for having allowed them to reach a site that is significant to them because it marks the first step on the "Road to Paradise." The leader of the Sac and Fox, a headman named Mohosca, reminds his people that in this "delicious land," "if we are sorrowful [we] feel comforted, if ill become healed, if already breaking from the bonds of flesh set out at once on the way to paradise instead of waiting."[13]

Quickly, however, it becomes clear that the joy the Sac and Fox feel about their arrival at this sacred site is threatened by an unknown menace that one old woman speculates could possibly be a demon, a maligned ghost, or the dreaded paleface. This impending threat has cast such a dark shadow over the tribe that it has thrown all aspects of Sac and Fox life out of balance. The tribal council despairs because the bright prophetic visions that the shaman Nana-by-yeh hoped to receive in the Sacred Hills have not appeared. Likewise, Kah-mee, the river god, has not spoken to the people as he had in previous years, perhaps, they reason, because the palefaces' puffing fireboats have forced him to move deeper in the Missouri River or farther upstream. Despite the darkness that hangs over the people, Mohosca encourages them to proceed with the celebration of the annual Green Corn feast. "A gloomy green-corn feast would be more terrible than anything that has heretofore befallen us," he tells his council.[14]

Against this bleak backdrop, love blossoms between two of the play's main characters, Talinka, a young Sac and Fox woman, and the tribe's war chief Cahaquas. As the two declare their affections for each other, they contemplate the uncertainty of the future that lays before them. They learn that the state of Missouri plans to annex the Platte country, the strip of land on which the Sacred Council Hills stand. As part of the treaty they signed with the U.S. government, the Sac and Fox must move across the river and leave the Sacred Hills forever. "Ever towards the setting sun they push us," Talinka laments. To this the love-struck Cahaquas replies, "Welcome banishment, welcome privation, the strange new life in the strange new land, if only we're together."[15]

The Sacred Council Hills ends as it began, with the Sac and Fox people on the move. This time, however, their hearts are heavy and they chant as they march off stage, away from the sacred hills:

> Farewell, farewell, oh, beautiful Hills farewell!
> With ax and with brand will [the palefaces] torture the land,
> Your groves, once so sacred no longer may stand . . .
> The paleface comes hither in blindness to dwell.
> Oh, beautiful Hills farewell.[16]

As the chant subsides, Owen's stage directions call for the strains of *Gloria in Excelsis* to rise in its wake.

Though European American characters do not appear in *The Sacred Council Hills*, their presence weighs heavily on the play's plot and in the hearts of its native characters. Likewise, the specter of death, though unseen, plays a central role in the melodrama. By consistently referring to whites as *pale*faces and equating them with demons and ghosts, Owen's Sac and Fox characters see whites as a plague that brings death to native people and destroy their land.

Curiously, though they are pursued by death, the Sac and Fox in Owen's play seem unable to defend themselves. Defeated and resigned, their only response to the threat that stalks them is to move, as Talinka says, "ever towards the setting sun." In fact, as the play opens, we sense that the Sac and Fox have already been moving for some time. By portraying their relief and gratitude at reaching the Sacred Hills, Owen leads us to believe that they have traveled a great distance. Though they had hoped to find rest, refuge, or even a dignified place to die in the hills that had comforted them in the past, they cannot. An irrepressible force pushes the Sac and Fox people toward their new homes on the west side of the Missouri River. In *The Sacred Council Hills*, Owen presents the removal of the Sac and Fox from the Platte Purchase region as an inevitable part of the white settlement of Missouri. Clearly, there is no place for these people in the new state that will be inhabited by European

Americans. Their removal across the river renders them invisible and their disappearance reinforces their mythical status as Vanishing Indians.

On December 16, 1911, Mary's mother Agnes Cargill Owen died at the family home on Ninth Street. She was eighty-one years old, and the *St. Joseph Gazette* claimed that at the time of her death, she had been the oldest of the city's remaining "original settlers."[17] "Every one's mother is 'best' to her children," Owen had once written to Leland, "but mine is really sanctified by her suffering and patience. She was accounted the most beautiful girl in Missouri, and her youthful associates could never explain the existence of her ugly duck called 'Mary.'"[18] While Owen adored her mother, her statement seems to indicate that she felt that she had never lived up to the ideals that she believed her mother embodied, especially in terms of beauty. But if Agnes Owen was beautiful, she also seems to have been a woman of strong fortitude. She had endured life in St. Joseph when it was little more than a pioneer settlement. Though her family had been wealthy, they were severely tested during the Civil War years. Through those difficult times, Agnes Owen had helped keep the family together while making sure that her children received an education, even when local schools were closed. Later, when the Radical Republicans and their Iron Clad Oath had hindered her husband's business interests, the family relied on her inheritance to maintain their lifestyle. Agnes Owen had encouraged each of her children to excel in the careers they had chosen, and, even in her later years as a housebound invalid, she remained the strong matriarch.

While her mother's death must have been a blow, it also freed Owen from some of her obligations and allowed her more time to travel for conferences and speeches. In 1911, Owen was still a highly regarded folklorist who remained in the public eye. She was occasionally profiled in newspaper pieces as the world's foremost expert in Indians, voodoo, and gypsies. "Miss Mary Alicia Owen is simply folklore, spelled another way," proclaimed an article in the Tacoma, Washington, *Times*.[19]

The following year, Owen made what was to be her final trip to Europe to present a paper on "The Rain Gods of the American Indians" in early September at the International Congress for the History of Religion in Leiden, Holland. Little is known about the trip, though Jean Fahey Eberle maintains that Owen traveled to Italy, France, Germany, and England to visit old acquaintances and perhaps to attend a folklore meeting in London. By November, she was back in St. Joseph to attend the wedding of a nephew and to complete the sizeable task of sorting through her mother's vast collection of papers, books, and clothing.[20]

Over the next decade, Owen devoted much of her energy to the Missouri Folk-Lore Society and a smaller folklore society that she helped organize in St. Joseph. Neither organization ever managed to attract many members. The Missouri Folk-Lore Society peaked at sixty-three members in 1910 while its local St. Joseph affiliate claimed a membership of about twenty-five.[21] Nonetheless, Owen poured a great deal of energy into the small but enthusiastic organizations. As president of the Missouri Folk-Lore Society, she attended annual meetings in St, Louis, Columbia, and Kansas City. At the tenth annual meeting in St. Louis in November 1916, she delivered a paper she had written on "The Folklore of Flowers that Grow in Missouri."

Owen's work with the St. Joseph Folk-Lore Society led to the publication of "Legends of St. Joseph," under her own name in the *St. Joseph Gazette* in December 1916. In her introduction to the legends, Owen wrote that the society planned to publish a book of local lore and was in the process of collecting stories. "The work is far from complete," she wrote. "Some of the material is fragmentary, some is really chaotic. Seldom is a tale given with the detail and precision with which the grandparents or parents of the narrator would have related it." Owen wrote that much of St. Joseph's folklore had already been lost and appealed to readers to send in their stories and folklore before they too were forgotten forever. Her sense of urgency was not without merit. It had been seven decades since the town of St. Joseph had been founded. Few of the residents who witnessed the town's early transformation from frontier trading post to urban boomtown were still living.[22] Owen wanted to record the stories of that process while it was still possible to do so.

Aside from her professional interest in the topic, Owen had a personal motive for collecting and presenting the folklore of her hometown. Much of St. Joseph's growth had occurred during her lifetime, and she had witnessed many of the changes the city had undergone since its founding. As she grew older, she no doubt felt a sense of nostalgia for the small muddy river town she had known as a child. As we have seen, she recreated that village more than once in her writing. "The Taming of Tarias" and *The Daughter of Alouette* both take place in the St. Joseph of the 1840s and 1850s. That earlier version of her hometown clearly had deep meaning for Owen, and she worked to record as much of its folklore as she could.

Her "Legends of St. Joseph" included eight different tales, several of which included American Indian characters. Interestingly, only one of the stories is likely to have come from Indian oral tradition. The rest were tales that originated among whites. "The Stone Woman" was a story Owen claimed to have collected from Indians on the Nemaha Reservation in Kansas. It told the story of a beautiful, wicked Indian woman who turned into stone because of her bad deeds. Another story told of a golden-haired ghost that wandered near King Hill, on St. Joseph's south side, after her Indian lover killed her. In "The Guardian of the Gold," the soul of an Indian boy watched protectively over a buried cache of gambler's gold. "The Poorhouse Ghost" is a twist on the ever-popular Indian captivity narrative. While captivity narratives usually involve white girls captured by Indians, this one is about an Indian girl who is taken by settlers passing through St. Joseph on their way west. Years later the girl, by then a fully grown woman who went by the name of Lucy, returns to St. Joseph. Over time she is driven insane by her inability to locate her original family and finally dies at the county farm.

Owen nurtured local talent in writing and folklore in other venues. At the same time that she worked with the St. Joseph Folk-Lore Society, she also led a group called the Mary Alicia Owen Story Tellers League. In 1918, the league published at least thirteen installments of a serial story "The House of Thirteen Windows" in the *St. Joseph Observer* and *St. Joseph Weekly Review*. Each member of the league was responsible for writing one chapter of the saga, which was about a young girl named Martina who was left an orphan at a house with thirteen windows on the Amazonia road outside St. Joseph.[23] Her work with the storytellers may have inspired her to do some creative writing of her own. Later that year, Owen published a poem called "St. Joseph's Sweet Singer" in the *Observer*.[24]

By 1920, the discipline of folklore studies had changed significantly. No longer the domain of amateur enthusiasts like Owen and Charles Leland, the field had become increasingly academic in nature. In the process, the focus of folklore studies had shifted as well. According to folklore historian Simon Bronner, as American society became more modern, folklorists became less interested in "removed primitives," such as American Indians and African American conjurers. Thanks largely to the influence of the anthropologist Franz Boas, who taught at Columbia University, the study of so-called primitives had fallen under the purview of the field of anthropology. Folklorists of the early twentieth century became more interested in what Bronner calls the "nearby man of tradition," those people who still practiced dying traditions of arts and crafts, or who remembered ancients songs and stories.[25]

This shift in folklore may have contributed to the fact that by 1920, enthusiasm for the Missouri Folk-Lore Society had waned. The society's small membership was shrinking as the group met for what was to be its last meeting for many years in Kansas City on November 11. As president, Owen spoke to the gathering about "The Legends of the Goose." Even after it ceased to meet, the work of the society was not finished. Henry Belden was still working on the publication of *Ballads and Songs Collected by the Missouri Folk-Lore Society*. Progress on the publication proved to be slow, however, in part because Owen had not fulfilled her promise to provide folklore that was not related to songs and ballads for the book. According to Belden, Owen's inability to provide material for the book was due to her poor health.[26]

Poor health, however, did not prevent Owen from publishing two significant articles while she was in her late sixties and early seventies. In 1920, she published "Social Customs and Usages in Missouri during the Last Century" in the State Historical Society of Missouri's *Missouri Historical Review*. Owen had been active in the society since its inception in 1898 and she held the distinction of being its first lifetime member. The article recorded a variety of social customs related to entertaining guests, Fourth of July picnics, holidays, and weddings. "Social Customs and Usages" is notable because it contains nothing about the folklore for which she was known best, that of American Indians and African Americans. This nostalgic look at the antiquated customs of pioneer life in Missouri, with its focus on the "nearby men—and women—of tradition," may have been Owen's attempt to keep up with the changing nature of folklore studies.[27]

A second article that appeared the following year in a Kansas City journal called *The Midwest Bookman* proved to have a more lasting impact on Owen's legacy. In "The Road to Paradise," Owen elaborated on the theme that she had touched on a decade earlier in her play *The Sacred Council Hills*. In both works, she portrayed the hills around St. Joseph as a place of renewal and safety, where indigenous people can rest on their weary journey before moving on. In those hills, people of all Indian nations could meet for council without fear of being attacked. But while the weary Sac and Fox in *The Sacred Council Hills* resumed their journey to their new reservation in Kansas at the end of the play, those Owen discussed in "The Road to Paradise" traveled a different kind of road. Owen contends that in the time before white settlers moved into the hills, Indians of many nations came there to die. From those sacred hills, travelers began their journey across the sun bridge in the sky, to their final resting place in the Happy Hunting Ground.[28] As we will see, this article set the course for the way in which the removal of native people from the Platte Purchase was popularly portrayed for decades to come.

Throughout the early 1920s, Owen remained active in her community. In 1921, she helped start a St. Joseph branch of the Missouri Writer's Guild. Owen also took an active role in politics. Women had gained the right to vote with the ratification of the Nineteenth Amendment to the Constitution on August 18, 1920. Thirteen days later, Marie Byrum became the first woman in Missouri to cast a ballot in a local election in Hannibal. At that pivotal moment in politics, both Mary Owen and her sister-in-law Harriett Kearney Owen were active in the Buchannan County Democratic Women's Club. Harriet Owen served as president of the club in 1920 and supported the recruitment of women political candidates. In support of the party, Mary Owen traveled to eight Buchannan County towns and village in eleven days to stump for Democratic candidates on the eve of the 1922 off-year general election.[29]

But those speeches may have been among the last that Mary Alicia Owen gave in public. Owen, who had been in poor health for some time, appeared less frequently in public and rarely published articles or stories after her seventieth birthday in 1920. This is not to say that Owen's mind was dormant during the years that ill health confined to her home. As rheumatism often prevented her from holding a pen, Owen became increasingly reliant on others to publish the stories she had collected over her long life. In 1926, the *St. Joseph News-Press* reprinted abbreviated versions of two of the St. Joseph legends that the Mary Alicia Owen Story Tellers had first published in the *Observer* a decade earlier. To these stories was added one about the Long Ghost Road, a variant of the "Road to Paradise." Also added was "Doctor Betsy," a tale about a doctor who was so mean that nothing green ever grew on her grave.[30]

During Owen's last years, visitors and reporters wishing to speak with her found that while she was sometimes willing to entertain their questions, she was often unable or unwilling to meet with them directly. Around 1930, Kansas City businessman Robert M. Snyder visited the Owen home to consult with Mary about an obscure book he was trying to locate. "She had been confined to her bed for a long period and could not see visitors," he wrote. Owen would not meet with Snyder but enlisted one of her sisters to act as an intermediary between the two. Though she was not able to recall the book Snyder was looking for, she asked her sister to relay to him a story she knew but had not published. It was the legend of "Apple Mary," a white captive that Joseph Robidoux's youngest son was said to have purchased from a group of Indians for a few bushels of apples. "She was willing for someone else to utilize the material," wrote Snyder, "the inference being that she would never again be able to take up her pen."[31] In fact, Owen did eventually use the story. An extended version of the tale of "Apple Mary" appeared in a St. Joseph newspaper—probably the *Observer*—as "Love Story of Faraon, Most Carefree of the Robidoux Boys." Highly reminiscent of "The Taming of Tarias" and *The Daughter of Alouette* in its romantic tone and its use of local color, "Love Story of Faraon" may have been one of the last stories Owen published.[32]

A few visitors did have the opportunity to visit Mary face-to-face, even though it sometimes meant that she had to greet them from her bed. One feature writer—perhaps Owen's friend Charles K. Soper—spent many hours with Owen during her final years and left an account of conversations he had with her. "There were times when she had great difficulty in talking, since she suffered for years with asthma, and I would suggest that I leave and come back another day," recalled the writer, "but she would keep me and continue her story. . . . My last afternoon with her alarmed me, for she could scarcely talk, her voice was husky and her asthma was very bad."[33]

In 1931, Owen discussed her failing health in her letter to the Missouri State Museum's A. C. Burrill. In large words scrawled across the pages of the letter, she wrote, "My aches are hard to bear if I try to talk. I can't get any better. No use to say I'd do differently if I had another chance. With the same temperament I'd do just the same, of course, but I wish I'd written down more accounts of experiences."

Her correspondence with Burrill was prompted by her donation of 226 items of Sac and Fox beadwork, clothing, and ceremonial objects to the museum. "I would like to feel that my precious ornaments were safely housed," Owen was quoted as saying after the state received her gift. "They can never be duplicated as they belong to a past even the red men are forgetting." To commemorate the receipt of the extraordinary collection, the museum mounted a display of many of the artifacts at the state capitol building. Writing about the exhibition in *Missouri* magazine, Mabel D. Thompson echoed Owen's belief that the display gave visitors an opportunity to see the handiwork of a vanishing people. The Sac and Fox "today would be utterly incapable of making such things." Those few who remained were "survivors of a tribe whose history is one of many trials and defeats but who struggled nobly to save their ancient customs from the onslaught of civilization as we know it today."[34]

On May 31, 1932, Mary Owen's sister Luella died in the family home in the company of her siblings. She had been ill for several months and succumbed to pneumonia at the age of eighty. Her obituary in the *St. Joseph News-Press* described her as the city's "most noted scientist," and listed many of her achievements in geology. The paper made note of the fact that Luella, like her sister Mary, had done some of her most important work—her groundbreaking research on loess soil—close to home. "Any description of Miss Owen," the *News-Press* continued, "would be incomplete without mention of the two sisters with whom she spent her life. . . . They have been noted for a lively and keen sense of humor and for graciousness."[35]

After Luella's death, Mary and Juliette lived alone in the house that, in their youth, had been home to a family of seven. Though the house and the lot in which it stood had remained largely unchanged over the decades the sisters had lived there, the surrounding neighborhood had changed significantly. By 1930, the property, which had once been located on the outer edge of St. Joseph, was within a few short blocks of the commercial district of a city that had grown to a population of seventy thousand people. In 1909, a large stone Methodist Episcopal church, known as the White Temple, was built on the northwest corner of the block on which the Owen sisters lived. By 1930, another large church building loomed over them from the lot just north of their house. The single-family homes and large yards that had once characterized the area around Ninth and Jules Streets had, by the 1930s, been replaced by brick row houses, apartments, and small businesses.[36]

Still, the sisters never seemed to consider moving. Juliette had been born in the house and Mary had lived there since the age of nine. To ease their situation, Mary hired a woman named Rose Hales to be her private nurse in 1933. While Hales attended to Owen's

Juliette Owen, left, and Mary Alicia Owen standing on the south side of the Owen home, c. 1900. Mary Alicia Owen was nine years old when this house, which was located at 306 North Ninth Street in St. Joseph, was built in 1859. This house served as the center of Owen's family and professional life until she died there in 1935. (Courtesy of the St. Joseph Historical Society)

physical care, she spent much of her time working as her personal secretary. In the final years of her life, Owen was said to have been working on a history of St. Joseph. However, in typical fashion, she had several projects going at once and Hales often traveled the two blocks to the public library to look up various bits of information. In quieter moments, Hales would read to Owen from texts on such diverse topics as politics, aviation, ancient history, and nursing.[37]

In late 1934, as Owen sensed that her health was worsening, she and Hales spent several days preparing plans for her funeral. Owen planned for the service to be held in the parlor of the family home and for her body to be interred less than a mile away in the Owen family mausoleum at Mount Mora Cemetery. She drew up a list of thirty-five people that she wanted to be notified of her death. By then nearly eighty-five years of age, Mary was sadly aware that she had outlived several of the people she had wanted to be her honorary pallbearers. Though she settled on a list of fourteen pallbearers, she chose to revive a tradition from her family's slave-holding past and asked that six African American men carry her coffin to the mausoleum.[38]

At about 1:30 on the morning of Saturday, January 5, 1935, Mary Alicia Owen died in her sleep at home. Though she suffered from a variety of ailments, the official causes of her death were listed as bronchopneumonia and arteriosclerosis.[39] All day Saturday, a steady stream of well-wishers visited the Owen house. The *St. Joseph Gazette* reported that "limousines rolled up to the front door where men and women prominent in the city's life called to pay their respects." The paper characterized Owen as one of the city's "real pioneers," who would be remembered for "her charities and the friendly hand she was always willing to extend to those in need." The *St. Joseph News-Press* summed up the life of the woman who had kept company with American Indians, conjurers, gypsies, folklorists, and politicians when it wrote, "the most remarkable characteristic of Miss Owen was that her interest in people was as great as her interest in books and learning."[40]

Epilogue
"Ever Towards the Setting Sun They Push Us"

Now, more than three-quarters of a century after Mary Alicia Owen's death, nearly all of her short stories, poems, and writings on folklore have slipped into obscurity. Her early works of fiction are buried so deeply in bound volumes of out-of-print periodicals that even Owen's biographers have unearthed only her best-known story, "The Taming of Tarias." Indeed, if it were not for the diligent work of digital librarians and archivists, who have scanned and indexed back issues of some of the journals, these works would remain largely inaccessible today. None of the books Owen wrote are available today in anything other than their rare original editions or in facsimile reprints. While a few scholars have cited her best-known books *Folk-Lore of the Musquakie Indians* and *Old Rabbit, the Voodoo, and Other Sorcerers* in their work, her novel *The Daughter of Alouette* and play *The Sacred Council Hills* are almost completely forgotten.

Folklorist and historian William K. McNeil speculated that Owen's association with Charles Leland was to blame for much of her current obscurity. Though Leland was American by birth, he lived much of his life in Europe and was associated with European rather than with American folklore circles. While Leland was able to assist Owen in many ways, his influence was largely European in nature. Through his professional connections, he helped her secure publishing contracts with British publishing houses. *Old Rabbit, the Voodoo, and Other Sorcerers* was published in the United States, but only after it had initially been printed in England. *The Sacred*

Council Hills was also published in the United States, but Owen published that work herself. Because British imprints distributed most of her work, writes McNeil, "Owen's influence was less extensive in the United States than it otherwise might have been."[1]

McNeil also puts some of the blame for Owen's obscurity on the fact that much of her scholarship now seems dated. As we have seen, many of the assumptions on which Owen based her works in folklore were grounded in academic theories and practices that today seem overtly racist. Indeed, though she possessed a curious mind and a quick intellect, she was very much a product of her time.

Despite her obscurity, however, two of Owen's articles resonate with many of those who are interested in Missouri history and folklore today. McNeil republished her 1920 essay "Social Customs and Usages in Missouri during the Last Century" in his 1984 anthology of Arkansas and Missouri folklore, *The Charm Is Broken*. More recently, the State Historical Society of Missouri reprinted it in an anthology of articles from the *Missouri Historical Review*.[2] That article remains a valuable resource because of its discussion of etiquette, customs, and pastimes that were common in Missouri in the nineteenth century.

However, the article that perhaps remains the most fixed in the popular imagination at the beginning of the twenty-first century is Owen's 1921 "The Road to Paradise." The city of St. Joseph has recently reprinted "The Road to Paradise" in booklet form, and it has become the foundation of a PowerPoint slide presentation that has been given by members of the St. Joseph Parks, Recreation, and Civic Facilities Department and is the subject of at least one work of public art in the city.[3]

In this article, Owen wrote that indigenous people believed the Blacksnake Hills around St. Joseph were sacred because they marked the beginning of the Road to Paradise that leads to the Happy Hunting Ground. The legend apparently started when settlers began to construct the town of St. Joseph in the bluffs overlooking the Missouri River. As they leveled hills and dug footings for new buildings, builders encountered a large number of native graves. The various configurations of these internments—scaffolds, stone crypts, and earth burials—led settlers to deduce that people of many different indigenous cultures had made them. Settlers theorized that native people from many regions must have traveled great distances to die in the hills so that they might be near the place where their journey to the afterlife was to begin.

"It was good to sojourn here," Owen wrote in "The Road to Paradise." "The Indian of any tribe drew his last sigh beside the Missouri, in as happy confidence in his beatitude as the East Indian has today on the banks of the Ganges. . . . I have enough of an Indian spirit myself to feel that heaven is a little nearer and a little surer here than elsewhere."[4]

While Owen's pronouncement may have been true, there is reason to be skeptical about the authenticity of the legend. What the region's nineteenth-century white settlers apparently failed to consider was that the archaeological riches they found in the hills around St. Joseph had not all been deposited recently. Instead, they were the remains of humans who had been interred there over many centuries. Evidence suggests that humans had inhabited present-day Missouri as early as 9250 B.C. Over the centuries, various indigenous cultures passed through the region. Each practiced different burial customs and left behind the various styles of graves that the settlers uncovered.[5]

Even in historic times, a single Indian nation might employ more than one burial procedure. Ethnographer Alanson Skinner, who worked with the Sac and Fox two decades after Owen, found that both the Ioway and the Sac and Fox used various practices, from placing bodies on scaffolds to burying them in the earth. Even earth burials could vary in their configuration. Skinner wrote that the clan of the deceased often dictated the manner in which a body was to be interred. Some chose to bury the body in a supine position while other might place it in a sitting position. Sometimes the Ioway laid a deceased person on the ground in a seated position and erected a small shelter of wood over the body.[6] It is not difficult to see how these various burial customs might have led settlers to conclude that they indicated that a great many cultures had visited to lay their dead to rest in the Blacksnake Hills.

There is also some question as to whether native people believed that the Blacksnake Hills was the location of the beginning of the Road to Paradise. Owen herself admitted that there was "no fragment of history chanted by the dying council fires of the red men," that recorded their belief in the legend of the Road to Paradise. "All that we know with certainty," she wrote, "is that the pioneers had it from the Indians." According to Skinner, the Ioway did believe that the souls of the dead traveled along what he called "the Road of the Dead" to a spirit town located in the western heavens. "Just before the soul reached the other world, it had to cross a river, after which it was received by its relatives who were already there." However, Skinner makes no reference to the road being associated with the Blacksnake Hills or any other specific geographical location.[7]

Nonetheless, the legend of the Road to Paradise has remained popular, finding its way into books, articles, and even into works of art. More than a decade before Owen wrote "The Road to Paradise," she had popularized the legend for the stage in her 1909 play, *The Sacred Council Hills*. In 1926, Owen's friend Charles K. Soper published an article about the Road to Paradise in the *Missouri Historical Review*. Soper used his article to delve deeper into the historical and archaeological record in an attempt to verify the legend. He discussed the various types of burials found in the St. Joseph region in more detail than Owen had. Soper also cited an unnamed source that claimed to have witnessed a party of what were believed to be Indians from the southwestern United States who had traveled to St. Joseph in 1860 for the express purpose of being buried there.[8]

In the 1920s, artist Bert G. Phillips made the legend the subject of a mural that he painted for the new Missouri State Capitol building in Jefferson City. According to the 1928 Report of the Missouri State Capitol Decoration Commission, Phillips's *Trail to the Happy Hunting Ground* shows that "from all points of the compass the Indians journeyed thither bearing their sick and dying that their journey to the 'Teepee in the Sun' might be short and easy." The painting depicts what appears to be a small Indian camp beside the Missouri River. In the right background are the hills that would one day become the site of St. Joseph. On the left side, across the river, are the river bluffs of present-day Kansas. In the far left of the painting, we see a woman with a baby in her arms facing away from the viewer, towards the river. According to the commission report, she is making "her first step on her way to the unknown. Her husband entreats her to remain, but neither his words, nor the grief for her stricken mother [at whom the husband gestures] seem able to detain her." She is about to break her bonds with this world to travel to the Teepee in the Sun, which is clearly seen in the sky at the painting's center.[9]

Bert G. Phillips, *Trail to the Happy Hunting Grounds*, c. early 1920s. This mural, which is in the Missouri State Capitol in Jefferson City, appears to have been inspired by Mary Alicia Owen's 1921 article "The Road to Paradise." It shows an American Indian camp on the banks of the Missouri River. The woman at the far left turns her back on her grieving family as she prepares to cross the river and begin her journey to the "Great Teepee in the Sky." (Photograph by the author)

More than four decades after Owen's death, St. Joseph historian Sheridan Logan revisited the legend in the opening pages *Old St. Jo,* a book he wrote about the city's history.

> The Blacksnake Hills were regarded by the [Indians] as sacred ground. . . . The gods had once dwelt there; the soil was so sacred that ailing chiefs of different tribes were brought great distances by travois to die there. They could be buried on the summits of the hills facing west over the valley of the Great River. The sunsets from those hills were so fine that Indians believed the rays of the setting sun provided an invisible bridge over which the souls of the departed took the direct road to Paradise and the Happy Hunting Grounds.[10]

More recently, Anthony Benton Gude, the grandson of famed regionalist painter Thomas Hart Benton, made the legend the subject of a 1997 mural he painted for a St. Joseph casino. *Chief White*

Cloud and the Legend of the Sun Bridge shows the Ioway leader Francis White Cloud on his knees atop a bluff overlooking the Missouri River. Accompanied by a pair of wolves, he gazes across the river, toward a sun bridge, an optical illusion that is created when the last rays of the setting sun spread across the landscape. In the sky, over White Cloud's head, Gude depicts native warriors in the clouds. Mounted on horseback, these warriors ride toward the sun bridge, apparently traveling to the next world.

Gude's painting is particularly noteworthy because of the way in which he has connected the legend of the sun bridge, or the Road to Paradise, with the removal of the Ioway and the Sac and Fox from Missouri in 1837. He did so by cleverly linking that story with Francis White Cloud and another popular legend having to do with a plant called plantain, or white man's foot. The son of a much-revered Ioway leader, Francis White Cloud assumed a leadership role among the Ioway after his father's death in 1834 and was one of the headmen who signed the Platte Purchase agreement two years later. According to the legend, White Cloud was greatly troubled about the prospect of selling the Ioways' last remaining land in Missouri to the United States. One day he climbed to the top of a bluff along the river—said to be King Hill in south St. Joseph—to pray for guidance. Upon reaching the top of the bluff, he noticed a weed called plantain growing there in abundance.

While more than one plant is known by the popular name plantain, the one associated with this legend, *Plantago major*, is not native to North America. European immigrants brought it with them to this continent because it was a valuable treatment for such wide-ranging ailments as epilepsy, sores, hemorrhoids, ulcers, earache, and toothache. It earned the name white man's foot, or Englishman's foot, because once it was introduced to the North American continent, it became an invasive species that spread quickly, like the white settlers. Seeing the plant growing at his feet, Francis White Cloud is said to have realized that the settlers' possession of the land was as inevitable as the growth of plantain and that it was time for him to cede it to the United States and move his people west, across the river.

In Gude's depiction of the scene, the wolves sit on White Cloud's right to symbolize the natural world. The plantain plant that he holds in his left hand, which grows along the top of the bluff on his

Anthony Benton Gude, *Chief White Cloud and the Legend of the Sun Bridge*, 1997, oil on canvas, 6 feet high x 16 feet wide. This mural, originally commissioned for a St. Joseph casino, depicts the moment at which Francis White Cloud decides to sign the Platte Purchase treaty in 1836. In his right hand, White Cloud holds plantain, also known as white man's foot. In the clouds above his head, native warriors cross the sky toward the sun bridge that will take them to the Happy Hunting Ground in the next world. (Courtesy of the artist)

left side, represents the encroaching white man. Another sign of the coming of civilization can be seen in the form of a small steamboat that chugs up the river in the left center of the painting. The painting is particularly poignant because the wolves and White Cloud gaze to the west in the direction that they too must travel to make way for the newly arrived settlers. In a sense, though they are not dead, they must travel a road that parallels the Road to Paradise as they are removed west of the river to Kansas.

Just as it has embraced the legend of the Road to Paradise in its interpretation of the city's history, St. Joseph has perpetuated the story of white man's foot in a sculpture the city recently commissioned to commemorate the Platte Purchase. In 2004, sculptor Claudia Packer created a life-sized bronze sculpture of Francis White Cloud that now stands near King Hill in a prominent location across the street from the entrance to the city's Hyde Park. *Chief White Cloud* depicts the Ioway leader at the crucial moment he resolved to sign the Platte Purchase treaty. In his right hand, Packer's White Cloud holds a plantain plant, which in this case symbolizes peace. In his left hand is a spear, which is meant to symbolize war. In this portrait, the Ioway leader can be seen weighing the options that are open to him. "It was an easy decision for the St. Joseph Parks, Recreation and Civic Facilities Department to choose to honor Chief White Cloud, Mahaska, with a bronze statue," states the program from the sculpture's unveiling. "It is his personal struggle with a difficult decision, and how he sought to find an answer which can parallel our own lives today."[11]

If White Cloud's dilemma and the story of white man's foot sounds familiar, consider that a variant of the story appeared in Henry Wadsworth Longfellow's enormously popular epic poem *The Song of Hiawatha* only two decades after the Platte Purchase treaty was signed. White man's foot is mentioned near the end of the poem as the hero Hiawatha prepares to depart his home on the shores of Gitche Gumee. Hiawatha has seen the signs of European American settlement in the appearance of the stinging bee and the blossoming plantain, and is convinced that it is time to move on. Like White Cloud, he crosses the water and moves "Westward, westward Hiawatha / Sailed into the fiery sunset / Sailed into the purple vapors / Sailed into the dusk of evening."[12]

Claudia Packer, *Chief White Cloud*, c. 2004, bronze, St. Joseph, Missouri. The Ioway leader Francis White Cloud was one of the signers of the Platte Purchase treaty of 1836, which ceded the last portion of Ioway land in the present-day state of Missouri to the United States. According to legend, White Cloud decided to sell the land when he saw that it was covered with plantain, also called white man's foot. The plant had been transplanted by Europeans when they settled on the North American continent and seemed to spread as quickly as white people did. In this portrait of White Cloud, Claudia Packer portrayed him with plantain leaves in his left hand. (Photograph by the author)

Both the legend of White Man's Foot and the Road to Paradise perpetuate the prevailing nineteenth- and early twentieth-century belief that American Indians were a vanishing race. In the rush to fulfill their Manifest Destiny, European Americans had forced native people and the North American wilderness to near extinction. Historian Jean M. O'Brien has written extensively about narratives like "The Road to Paradise" and the legend of White Man's Foot, in which European American writers make Indian people vanish. In her study of hundreds of local histories written in southern New England in the nineteenth century, O'Brien found that for most, the story of a place began only at the moment that white pioneers set foot on it. While such histories often included an obligatory paragraph or two that made a vague reference to the aboriginal people who had once called the place home, far more space was devoted to lists of European "firsts" that had taken place there. Almost uniformly these lists included, but were not limited to, first white settlers, first white babies, first newspapers, first churches, and first schools. O'Brien has referred to this as "firsting," and notes that this process of creating these lists allowed settlers to claim Indian places as their own.[13]

O'Brien has found that settlers believed these "firsts" were necessary because Indians had failed to live up to man's divine assignment to domesticate and subdue the earth. Because of this failure, the authors of local histories often posited that European Americans, who were better prepared to undertake the task of civilizing the land, had justifiably supplanted native people. O'Brien refers to the process of justifying this expulsion as "replacing."

In a sense, legends like the Road to Paradise and White Man's Foot serve the same purpose as the local histories about which O'Brien writes. They offer one view of the process by which European American replaced American Indians in St. Joseph. If Mary Alicia Owen felt a sense of guilt over the removal of Indians from the Blacksnake Hills, these replacement narratives helped to ease that guilt by adding a sense of inevitability to it. The legends of White Man's Foot and the Road to Paradise recount the removal of native people from Missouri's borders in a way that is free of confrontation and violence. In these stories, Indian people choose to leave their land of their own accord, if reluctantly. They assure whites that while the Ioway and the Sac and Fox had to leave a homeland that ended at the banks of the Missouri River, they only made the "short and easy" journey along the Road to Paradise, to the happy hunting ground that awaited them on the opposite shore.

$\mathcal{N}otes$

Introduction

1. "Old Owen Home, Built in 1860, Being Demolished," *St. Joseph News-Press*, 26 May 1948, newspaper clipping, vertical file: St. Joseph—Biography—Owen Family, St. Joseph Public Library, St. Joseph, Missouri.
2. "Owen House Has Stayed One Step Ahead of the World," *St. Joseph News-Press*, undated newspaper clipping, vertical file: St. Joseph—Biography—Owen Family, St. Joseph Public Library.
3. "Friends Pay Tribute to Miss Owen," *St. Joseph Gazette*, 6 October 1935, 2A.
4. "Juliette Owen, Pioneer, Dead," *St. Joseph Gazette*, 26 October 1943; "Nephew of Miss Owen to Handle Her Estate," 31 October 1948, newspaper clippings, vertical file: St. Joseph—Biography—Owen Family, St. Joseph Public Library.
5. The people Mary Alicia Owen referred to collectively as the Musquakie (today commonly spelled Meskwaki) are actually three distinct tribal nations, the Sac and Fox Nation of Oklahoma, the Sac and Fox Nation of Missouri in Kansas and Nebraska and the Sac and Fox Tribe of the Mississippi in Iowa. This last nation is still commonly referred to as the Meskwaki.
6. Jean Fahey Eberle, *The Incredible Owen Girls* (St. Louis: Boar's Head Press, 1977); Doris Land Mueller, *Daring to Be Different: Missouri's Remarkable Owen Sisters* (Columbia: University of Missouri Press, 2010); William K. McNeil "Mary Alicia Owen, Collection of Afro-American and Indian Lore in Missouri," *Missouri Folklore Society Journal* 2 (1980): 1–14; Mary Elizabeth Allcorn, "Mary Alicia Owen: Missouri Folklorist," *Missouri Folklore Society Journal* 8–9 (1986–1987): 71–78.
7. Alison K. Brown, "Beads, Belts, and Bands: The Mesquakie Collection of Mary Alicia Owen," *Missouri Folklore Society Journal* 18–19 (1996–1997): 25–44; Alison K. Brown, "Collecting Material Folklore: Motivations and Methods in the Owen and Hasluck Collections," *Folklore* 109 (1998): 33–40; Neil Schmitz, *White Robe's Dilemma: Tribal History in American Literature* (Amherst: University of Massachusetts, 2001); David Murray, *Matter,*

Magic, and Spirit: Representing Indian and African American Belief (Philadelphia: University of Pennsylvania Press, 2007); Jeffrey E. Anderson, *Conjure
in African American Society* (Baton Rouge: Louisiana State University Press,
2005).

8. Eberle, *The Incredible Owen Girls*, 42; Alcorn, "Mary Alicia Owen: Missouri Folklorist," 72.

9. Robert L. Carneiro, *Evolutionism in Cultural Anthropology* (Boulder,
CO: Westview Press, 2003): 21; Curtis M. Hinsley Jr., *Savages and Scientists:
The Smithsonian Institution and the Development of American Anthropology,
1846–1910* (Washington, DC: Smithsonian Institution Press, 1981): 125; Ste-
phen K. Sanderson, *Social Evolutionism: A Critical History* (Cambridge, MA:
Blackwell, 1990): 10–16.

10. "Famous in Folklore," *Hopkinsville Kentuckian*, 1 February 1895, 4.

11. Renato Rosaldo, *Culture and Truth: The Remaking of Social Analysis*
(Boston: Beacon Press, 1993): 30; Schmitz, *White Robe's Dilemma*, 68.

Chapter 1

1. Mary Alicia Owen to Charles Godfrey Leland, 25 June 1893, 21 March
1895, 29 June 1898, Owen, Mary Alicia (to Charles Leland), Historical Society of Pennsylvania Society small collection (collection 22B), Historical
Society of Pennsylvania.

2. J. N. B. Hewitt, ed., *Journal of Rudolph Friederich Kurz* (Lincoln: University of Nebraska Press, 1970): 66–67; case file index, St. Louis Circuit Court
files, Missouri State Archives–St. Louis.

3. Louise Barry, *The Beginning of the West: Annals of the Kansas Gateway
to the American West, 1540–1854* (Topeka: Kansas State Historical Society,
1972), 78, 133; Robert J. Willoughby, *Robidoux's Town: A Nineteenth-Century
History of St. Joseph, Missouri* (Westphalia, MO: Westphalia Printing, 1997),
6–9; *The History of Buchanan County, Missouri* (St. Joseph, MO: Union Historical Company, 1881), 392–95.

4. Willoughby, *Robidoux's Town*, 11; *The History of Buchanan County, Mis-
souri*, 394; Maximilian von Wied, "Maximilian, Prince of Wied's, Trav-
els in the Interior of North America, 1832–1834, Part I," in Reuben Gold
Thwaites, *Early Western Travels, 1748–1846*, vol. 22 (Cleveland: Arthur H.
Clark, 1906), 257; case file index, St. Louis Circuit Court, Missouri State
Archives–St. Louis.

5. Tanis Thorne, *The Many Hands of My Relations: French and Indians on the
Lower Missouri River* (Columbia: University of Missouri Press, 1996), 160–
65; Roy E. Coy and Mrs. Walter Hall, The Genealogy of the White Cloud
Family," *Museum Graphic* 9 (Spring 1952): 8.

6. "Treaty with the Oto, etc., 1836" and "Treaty with the Iowa, etc., 1836,"
in Charles J. Kappler, ed., *Indian Affairs: Laws and Treaties*, vol. 2 (Washington, DC: Government Printing Office, 1904), 468–70, 479–81.

7. *History of Buchanan County*, 396–98; Willoughby, *Robidoux's Town*, 16–17.

8. Willoughby, *Robidoux's Town*, 18–21; *History of Buchanan County*, 405.
Hewitt, ed., *Journal of Rudolph Friederich Kurz*, 53–54.

9. Sheridan A. Logan, *Old St. Jo: Gateway to the West, 1799–1932* (St. Joseph, MO[?]: John Sublett Logan Foundation, 1979), 210; Ada Lyon, "Cargill

Name Is Closely Connected with St. Joseph History," *St. Joseph News-Press*, 2 October 1949: 16A; Walter Williams, "James A. Owen Family," *History of Northwest Missouri*, vol. 2 (Chicago: Lewis, 1915), 671.

10. *1860 Missouri Agricultural Census* (State Historical Society of Missouri microfilm publication).

11. Logan, *Old Saint Jo*, 367; Floyd Calvin Shoemaker, ed., "James Alfred Owen," in *Missouri and Missourians: Land of Contrast and People of Achievements*, vol. 4 (Chicago: Lewis, 1943), 31–33.

12. Logan, *Old St. Jo*, 26.

13. Logan, *Old St. Jo*, 49.

14. Willoughby, *Robidoux's Town*, 31–38, 55–67; Eberle, *The Incredible Owen Girls*, 7.

15. Colonel M. F. Tiernan quoted in Willoughby, *Robidoux's Town*, 1.

16. Hewitt, ed., *The Journal of Rudolph Friedrich Kurz*, 36–37.

17. *Buchanan County and St. Joseph*, 202; Willoughby, *Robidoux's Town*, 84.

18. "Cargill Name Is Closely Connected with St. Joseph History," *St. Joseph News-Press*; "Missouri Slave Schedules," *Population Schedules of the Seventh Census of the United States* (National Archives Microfilm Publication M432, roll 422), United States Bureau of the Census; "Missouri Slave Schedules, vol. 1," *Population Schedules of the Eighth Census of the United States* (National Archives Microfilm Publication M653, roll 661), United States Bureau of the Census. Unfortunately, none of the slaves listed as belonging to the Owen or Cargill household are listed by name in the Slave Schedules.

19. A summary of Missouri slave freedom suits involving African American Indians can be seen at St. Louis Circuit Court Historical Records Project (http://www.stlcourtrecords.wustl.edu/about-freedom-suits-series.php #four, accessed 22 January 2011).

20. "A talk or council held with the chiefs and braves of the Iowa tribe of Indians by T. H. Harvey in the chapel at the mission in the Great Nemaha sub agency on the 14 April 1846," *Great Nemaha Agency Files* (National Archives Microfilm Publication M234, Roll 307), letter received by the Office of Indian Affairs, 1824–1881, Record Group 75; Willoughby, *Robidoux's Town*, 86.

21. Mary Alicia Owen, *Old Rabbit, the Voodoo, and Other Sorcerers* (1893; reprint, North Stratford, NH: Ayer, 1999), 10–11.

22. Mueller, *Daring to Be Different*, 47; Shoemaker, ed., *Missouri and Missourians*, vol. 4, 34; death certificates record Florence Owen's birth date as March 11, 1857, and Herbert Owen's as May 19, 1857. Clearly at least one of the certificates is erroneous. Other biographical sources list Herbert Owen's year of birth as 1857. Missouri death certificate database, Missouri State Archives (http://www.sos.mo.gov/archives/resources/deathcertificates/, accessed 7 January 2011).

23. "Cargill Name Is Closely Connected with St. Joseph History," *St. Joseph News-Press*.

24. Eberle, *The Incredible Owen Girls*, 14.

25. Mary Alicia Owen, "Among the Voodoos," in Joseph Jacobs and Alfred Nutt, eds., *The International Folk Lore Congress, 1891: Papers and Transactions*

(London: David Nutt, 1892), 230–48; Mueller, *Daring to Be Different*, 19; Sanborn map 8, 1883; map 17, 1888; map 43, 1897; map 44, 1911, "The Sanborn Fire Insurance Map Collection," *University of Missouri Digital Library* (Internet: http//digital.library.umsystem.edu/, accessed 16 November 2011); "1850 Missouri Census for Buchanan, Butler, Caldwell, and Callaway counties," *Population Schedules of the Seventh Census of the United States* (National Archives Microfilm Publication M432, roll 393), United States Bureau of the Census.

26. *Owen v. Ford et al.*, February term 1872, file ID# 159366, Missouri Supreme Court files, Missouri State Archives.

Chapter 2

1. Preston Filbert, *The Half Not Told: The Civil in a Frontier Town* (Mechanicsburg, PA: Stackpole Books, 2001), xi.

2. Logan, *Old Saint Jo*, 26, 368; Willoughby, *Robidoux's Town*, 69.

3. James A. Owen quoted in Logan, *Old Saint Jo*, 368. Owen's comments come from what has been referred to as his Civil War diary, the location of which Logan does not cite, even though he quotes from it extensively. At times, the "diary" reads more like a memoir that was written after the war. It is therefore possible that Logan's quotes come from an article Owen published after the war, perhaps in a newspaper or a volume of local history.

4. *Buchanan County and St. Joseph*, 203; Willoughby, *Robidoux's Town*, 98; Filbert, *The Half Not Told*, 21–23.

5. Willoughby, *Robidoux's Town*, 99; confession of Jessie C. Stovall, Jr., Livingston County, Missouri, December 1863, *Union Provost Marshals' File of Papers Relating to Individual Citizens, 1861–1866* (National Archives Microfilm M345 roll F1607), War Department Collection of Confederate Records, Record Group 109.

6. Willoughby, *Robidoux's Town*, 101.

7. "Guerrillas in Missouri: An Important Order by General Schofield," *New York Times*, 29 June 1862.

8. Excerpt from James Owen's diary quoted in Logan, *Old St. Jo*, 368; the Missouri State Archives Soldiers' Records Database shows that William R. Penick's Fifth Regiment Cavalry, Missouri State Volunteers were based in St. Joseph in 1862 (http://www.sos.mo.gov/archives/soldiers/0).

9. Logan, *Old St. Jo*, 369.

10. Letter from Albert Clark, 26 March 1864, Buchanan County, Missouri, *Union Provost Marshals' File* (National Archives Microfilm M345 roll F1607); Logan, *Old St. Jo*, 210.

11. Owen quoted in Logan, *Old St. Jo*, 368.

12. Owen quoted in Logan, *Old St. Jo*, 369; Filbert, *The Half Not Told*, 83–87.

13. Logan, *Old St. Jo*, 369–70.

14. David D. March, "Charles D. Drake and the Constitutional Convention of 1865," *The Civil War in Missouri: Essays from the Missouri Historical Review, 1906–2006* (Columbia: State Historical Society of Missouri, 2006), 208–24.

15. *Kansas City Journal of Commerce*, 24 October 1865, quoted in Willough-by, *Robidoux's Town*, 104.

16. LeeAnn Whites, *Gender Matters: Civil War, Reconstruction, and the Making of the New South* (New York: Palgrave MacMillan, 2005), 22, 23.

17. "Mary Alicia Owen, Noted Folklorist, Died This Morning." *St. Joseph News-Press*, 5 January 1935.

18. Eberle, *The Incredible Owen Girls*, 8–9, 21–22.

19. "1870 Missouri Census for Washington Township, Buchanan County, Missouri," *Population Schedules of the Eighth Census of the United States* (National Archives Microfilm Publication M593 roll 762), U.S. Bureau of the Census.

20. Eberle, *The Incredible Owen Girls*, 1–3.

21. Julia Scott [Mary Alicia Owen], "The Exile's Daughter," *Godey's Lady's Book and Magazine* 111, no. 663 (September 1885).

22. Matthew Vassar quoted in Sherbrooke Rogers, *Sarah Josepha Hale: A New England Pioneer, 1788–1879* (Grantham, NH: Tompson and Rutter, 1985), 103; Joan Marie Johnson, *Southern Women at Vassar: The Poppenheim Family Letters, 1882–1916* (Columbia: University of South Carolina Press, 2002), 4–5.

23. Sarah Josepha Hale to Matthew Vassar, 30 April 1860, in Edward R. Linner, *Vassar: The Remarkable Growth of a Man and His College, 1855–1865* (Poughkeepsie, NY: Vassar College, 1984), 114.

24. Hale to Vassar, 30 March 1865, in Linner, *Vassar*, 109.

25. Linner, *Vassar*, 129–41; Rogers, *Sarah Josepha Hale*, 103–11.

26. *Letters from Old Time Vassar: Written by a Student in 1869–1870* (Poughkeepsie, NY: Vassar College, 1915); Linner, *Vassar*, 54.

27. Ellen Swallow, 11 October 1968, quoted in Elizabeth Daniels, *History of Vassar College* (http://historian.vassar.edu/chronology/1861–1870, accessed 21 April 2009).

28. Letter by an unnamed Vassar student to an unnamed parent, 7 March 1870, in *Letters from Old Time Vassar*, 92–93.

29. Johnson, *Southern Women at Vassar*, 5, 7–11; Eberle, *The Incredible Owen Girls*, 27–29.

Chapter 3

1. Janice Brandone-Falcone, "Constance Runcie and the Runcie Club of St. Joseph," in Thomas M. Spencer, ed., *The Other Missouri History: Populists, Prostitutes, and Regular Folks* (Columbia: University of Missouri Press, 2004), 172–74.

2. Brandone-Falcone, "Constance Runcie and the Runcie Club of St. Joseph," 170.

3. "Wide Recognition for Folklorist Won by Retiring Missouri Woman," *Kansas City Star*, 24 January 1941; Logan, *Old St. Jo*, 367; Alcorn, "Mary Alicia Owen: Missouri Folklorist," 71; Mary Elizabeth Allcorn, "Mary Alicia Owen: Missouri Folklorist," 71; "George E. King," in *History of Buchanan County, Missouri*, 795–96.

4. Henry Nash Smith, "The Scribbling Women and the Cosmic Success Story," *Critical Inquiry* 1, no. 1 (September 1974): 58.

5. Julia Scott [Mary Alicia Owen], "Jack in Search of Jill," *Peterson's Magazine* 86, no. 3 (September 1884): 243.

6. Julia Scott [Mary Alicia Owen], "The Exile's Daughter," *Godey's Lady's Book and Magazine* 111, no. 663 (September 1885): 243.

7. Julia Scott [Mary Alicia Owen], "The New Tenor," *Frank Leslie's Popular Monthly* 29, no. 5 (May 1890): 609.

8. Henry Nash Smith, "The Scribbling Women," 64.

9. Bernd C. Peyer, *The Singing Spirit: Early Short Stories by North American Indians* (Tuscon: University of Arizona Press, 1989), xi; Henry Nash Smith, "The Scribbling Women," 65.

10. Mary Alicia Owen, "The Bride's Farewell," *Prairie Farmer* 41, no. 8 (26 February 1870): 62.

11. Julia Scott [Mary Alicia Owen], "Patty's Literary Experiences," *Ballou's Monthly Magazine* 60, no. 1 (July 1884): 83.

12. Julia Scott [Mary Alicia Owen], "Miss Dolly's Ideals," *Ballou's Monthly Magazine* 65, no. 6 (June 1887): 499.

13. Henry Nash Smith, "The Scribbling Women," 55.

14. Julia Scott [Mary Alicia Owen], "Phoebus or Cupid," *Overland Monthly* (August 1886): 129.

15. Mary Alicia Owen, "The Taming of Tarias," *The Century* 39, no. 2 (December 1889): 284–91.

16. Alan Trachtenberg, *The Incorporation of America: Culture and Society in the Gilded Age* (New York: Hill and Wang, 1982), 189–90; Henry Nash Smith, "The Scribbling Women," 65.

17. Logan, *Old Saint Jo*, 136–40.

18. Robert H. Wiebe, *The Search for Order, 1877–1920* (New York: Hill and Wang, 1995), 5, 12, 52, and 54.

19. Frederick Jackson Turner, "The Significance of the Frontier in American History," *The Frontier in American History* (New York: Dover, 1996), 1–38.

20. "James Alfred Owen," in Shoemaker, ed., *Missouri and Missourians*, 32.

Chapter 4

1. It is unclear whether Olivia Proctor was Richard Proctor's daughter or stepdaughter. An article that appeared in the *New York Times* after Proctor's death states that his five children were named Mary, John, Richard, Agnes, and Harry. An obituary in the *Monthly Notices of the Royal Astronomical Society* states, however, that Proctor had six children from his first marriage. It is possible that Olivia was the sixth child. See "R. A. Proctor's Body at Rest," *New York Times*, 4 October 1893; "Richard Anthony Proctor," *Monthly Notices of the Royal Astronomical Society* 49 (February 1889): 164–68; "St. Joe's Welcome to Professor Proctor," *New York Times*, 18 July 1884; "General Notes," *New York Times*, 3 May 1884; Eberle, *The Incredible Owen Girls*, 39.

2. Charles Godfrey Leland, *Memoirs*, vol. 1 (London: William Heinemann, 1894), 4.

3. Charles Godfrey Leland, *The Algonquin Legends of New England; Or, Myths and Folk Lore of the Micmac, Passamaquoddy, and Penobscot Tribes* (Boston: Houghton, Mifflin, 1884), 8.

4. Charles Leland to Mary Alicia Owen, 21 April 1889 and 7 June 1889, in Elizabeth Robins Pennell, *Charles Godfrey Leland: A Biography* (1906; reprint, Freeport, NY: Books for Libraries Press, 1970), 314–15.

5. Charles Godfrey Leland, introduction to Owen, *Old Rabbit*, viii.

6. Leland to Owen, 21 April 1889 and 7 June 1889, in Pennell, *Charles Godfrey Leland*, 314–16.

7. Anderson, *Conjure in African American Society*, 52–72.

8. Anderson, *Conjure in African American Society*, x–xi, 27–28.

9. Owen, "Among the Voodoos," 242.

10. Owen, "Among the Voodoos," 242.

11. Owen, "Among the Voodoos," 243.

12. Anderson, *Conjure in African American Society*, 37; Owen, *Old Rabbit*, 169.

13. Owen, *Old Rabbit*, 169–79; Owen, "Among the Voodoos," 232–33.

14. Leland to Owen, 22 July 1889, in Pennell, *Charles Godfrey Leland*, 320.

15. Leland to Owen, 22 October 1889, in Pennell, *Charles Godfrey Leland*, 322.

16. Leland to E. R. Pennell, 11 October 1891, in Pennell, *Charles Godfrey Leland*, 350.

17. Owen, "Among the Voodoos," 247–48.

18. Owen, "Among the Voodoos," 231, 243.

19. Owen, "Among the Voodoos," 231–32.

20. Owen, "Among the Voodoos," 232.

21. Owen, "Among the Voodoos," 232–36.

22. Owen, "Among the Voodoos," 244; Arthur McManus appears in the 1900 U.S. Census as a seventy-five-year-old head of household living on North Eighteenth Street in St. Joseph with a son and daughter. *Population Schedules of the Twelfth Census of the United States* (National Archives Microfilm Publication T623, roll 841, 84)**,** United States Bureau of the Census.

23. Owen, "Among the Voodoos," 246.

24. Mary Alicia Owen, "Voodooism," in Helen Wheeler Bassett and Frederick Star, eds., *The International Folk-Lore Congress of the World's Columbian Exposition* (Chicago: Charles H. Sergel, 1898), 325; Owen, "Among the Voodoos," 240.

25. Owen, "Voodooism," 325.

26. Owen, "Voodooism," 322.

27. Owen, "Voodooism," 236–41.

28. Owen, "Among the Voodoos," 236.

29. Owen, "Among the Voodoos," 239.

30. Owen to Leland, 20–27 September 1898, HSP.

31. Owen to Leland, undated, probably November or December 1898, HSP.

32. Owen to Leland, 20–27 September 1898, HSP.

33. Letter quoted in Anderson, *Conjure in African American Society*, 3.

34. Owen, "Among the Voodoos," 247–48.

35. Murray, *Matter, Magic, and Spirit*, 6.

36. Murray, *Matter, Magic, and Spirit*, 59; Mary Alicia Owen, "Hoodoo Luck Balls (Jack Balls)," in Catherine Yronwode, ed., *Ghostly Voices from Dixieland* (http://www.southern-spirits.com/owen-hoodoo-luck-balls.html, accessed 21 June 2011).

37. Leland to Owen, 23 July 1890, Pannell, *Charles Godfrey Leland*, 328.

38. Owen to Leland, 20 November 1895 and 27 November 1895, HSP.

39. Owen to Leland, 21 March 1895, 20 September 1898, HSP; Mueller, *Daring to Be Different*, 48.

40. Leland to Owen, 1 August 1890, in Pannell, *Charles Godfrey Leland*, 331.

41. Ibid.; Jay Hansford C. Vest, "From Bobtail to Brer Rabbit: Native American influences on Uncle Remus," *American Indian Quarterly* 24, no. 1 (winter 2000): 23–24.

42. Leland to Owen, 1 August 1890, Pannell, *Charles Godfrey Leland*, 331.

Chapter 5

1. Simon J. Bronner, *Folklife Studies from the Gilded Age: Object, Rite, and Custom in Victorian America* (Ann Arbor: UMI Research Press, 1987), 5, 7.

2. Aaron Garrett, "Anthropology: The Origin of Human Nature," in Alexander Brodie, ed., *The Cambridge Companion to the Scottish Enlightenment* (New York: Cambridge University Press, 2003), 79–80.

3. Sanderson, *Social Evolutionism*, 5.

4. Lewis Henry Morgan quoted in Carneiro, *Evolutionism in Cultural Anthropology*, 14–16.

5. Sanderson, *Social Evolutionism*, 13.

6. Rosemary Levy Zumwalt, *American Folklore Scholarship: A Dialogue of Dissent* (Bloomington: Indian University Press, 1988), 7, 99.

7. Zumwalt, *American Folklore Scholarship*, xii, 7.

8. Newell quoted in Zumwalt, *American Folklore Scholarship*, 13, 17.

9. "The International Folklore Congress, 1891," *Folk-Lore* 2, no. 3 (September 1891): 373.

10. "The International Folklore Congress, 1891," 374–78.

11. "International Folk-Lore Congress," *Times* (London), 6 October 1891, 8; Zumwalt, *American Folklore Scholarship*, 10.

12. Richard M. Dorson, "American Folklorists in Britain," *Journal of the Folklore Institute* 7, no. 2/3 (August–December 1970): 189.

13. Dorson, "American Folklorists in Britain," 191–92.

14. Owen to Leland, 24 July 1893 (HSP).

15. "International Folk-Lore Congress," *Times* (London), 6 October 1891, 8; Owen's speech was later published as "Among the Voodoos," in Joseph Jacobs and Alfred Nutt, eds. *The International Folk Lore Congress, 1891: Papers and Transactions* (London: David Nutt, 1892), 230–48.

16. Leland to E. R. Pennell, 11 October 1891, in Pennell, *Charles Godfrey Leland*, 350.

17. Leland, introduction to *Old Rabbit*, ix; Eberle, *The Incredible Owen Girls*, 48–49.

18. Simon J. Bronner, *American Folklore Studies: An Intellectual History* (Lawrence: University Press of Kansas, 1986), 35.

19. Brown, "Collecting Material Folklore," 34; Bronner, *American Folklore Studies*, 35–36.

20. Leland to E. R. Pennell, 11 October 1891, in Pennell, *Charles Godfrey Leland*, 352, 353–54.

21. "Negro-Folk Lore. Voodoo Tales. As Told among the Negroes of the Southwest," *New York Times*, 16 April 1893; "Stories of Negro Lore," *New York Sun*, 9 April 1893, 2.

22. "Negro-Folk Lore," *New York Times*, 16 April 1893; E. Sydney Heartland, review of *Old Rabbit, the Voodoo, and Other Sorcerers*, by Mary Alicia Owen, *Folklore* 5 (March 1894): 72–73.

23. Leland, introduction to *Old Rabbit*, v, vii; J[ames]. O[wen]. D[orsey], review of *Old Rabbit, the Voodoo, and Other Sorcerers*, by Mary Alicia Owen, *Journal of American Folklore* 6 (October–December 1893): 322–24.

24. Owen to Leland, 25 June 1893 (HSP).

25. Owen, "Voodooism," 313.

26. Zumwalt, *American Folklore Scholarship*, 24–28.

27. Zumwalt, *American Folklore Scholarship*, 27.

28. Fletcher Bassett, "Opening Address," in Bassett and Starr, eds., *The International Congress of the World's Columbian Exposition*, 18–19.

29. Owen, "Voodooism," 325.

30. Annah Robinson Watson, "Comparative Afro-American Folk-Lore," in Bassett and Star, eds., *The International Folk-Lore Congress of the World's Columbian Exposition*, 328.

31. "Some Clever Women," *Hocking Sentinel*, 14 February 1895, 1; "Famous in Folklore," *Hopkinsville Kentuckian*, 1 Feb 1895.

32. Correspondence, Leland to Owen, 25 February 1894, in Pennell, *Charles Godfrey Leland*, 372.

33. "Wide Recognition for Folklorist Won by Retiring Missouri Woman," *Kansas City Star*, 24 January 1941.

34. Eberle, *The Incredible Owen Girls*, 58–59; Mueller, *Daring to be Different*, 65.

35. Owen, "Among the Voodoos," 248, 239; correspondence, Owen to Leland, 25 June 1893 (HSP).

36. Mary Alicia Owen to Dr. A. C. Burrill, May 1931, photocopy of handwritten original, Rebecca and Adolph Schroeder Papers, collection WUNP 5643, Western Historical Manuscripts Collection–Columbia; "Famous in Folklore," *Hopkinsville Kentuckian*, 1 Feb 1895.

Chapter 6

1. Peyer, *The Singing Spirit*, viii–x.

2. Elizabeth Luther Cary, "Recent Writings by American Indians." *The Book Buyer* (1902, University of Virginia Library, http://etext.lib.virginia.edu/toc/modeng/public/CarRece.html, accessed 27 May 2009), 21–25.

3. Peyer, *The Singing Spirit*, vii; Karttunen, *Between Worlds*, 73–83.

4. "Antonio Apache Says He's No Negro," *New York Times*, 4 July 1907; "President Roosevelt's Day," *New York Times*, 25 July 1900.

5. Owen to Leland, 5 November 1898 (HSP).

6. Owen to Burrill, May 1931, WHMC-C; Eberle, *The Incredible Owen Girls*, 32.

7. Eberle, *The Incredible Owen Girls*, 32–37.

8. Mary Alicia Owen, *Folk-lore of the Musquakie Indians of North America and Catalogue of Musquakie Beadwork and Other Objects in the Collection of the Folk-Lore Society* (London: D. Nutt, 1904), 41; Owen to Burrill, May 1931, WHMC-C; Mary Alicia Owen, "The Road to Paradise," *Midwest Bookman* 3 (1921): 3–7.

9. Owen to Leland, 21 March 1895, (HSP).

10. Mary Alicia Owen, *The Daughter of Alouette* (London: Methuen, 1896), 137.

11. Owen, *The Daughter of Alouette*, 178–79.

12. Mohosca appears to be based on the Ioway leader Mahaska II, who was also known as Francis White Cloud (c. 1811–1859). Mahaska II was one of the headmen of the Ioway at the time the tribe moved to the Great Nemaha Reservation in Kansas in 1837. He married a mixed-blood woman, Mary "Many Days" Robidoux, the daughter of trader and founder of St. Joseph, Missouri, Joseph Robidoux. See Coy and Hill, "The Genealogy and History of the White Cloud Family," *Museum Graphic* 9 (Spring 1952); Martha Royce Blaine, *The Ioway Indians* (Norman: University of Oklahoma Press, 1995); and Thomas L. McKenney and James Hall, "Young Mahaska," *History of the Indian Tribes of North America*, vol. 2 (Philadelphia: D. Rice and A. N. Hart, 1855).

13. Owen, *The Daughter of Alouette*, 265.

14. Owen, *The Daughter of Alouette*, 295–96.

15. Owen, *The Daughter of Alouette*, 318–19.

16. Owen, *The Daughter of Alouette*, 322–23.

17. Ter Ellingson, *The Myth of the Noble Savage* (Berkley: University of California Press, 2001), 80–82.

18. Ellingson, *The Myth of the Noble Savage*, 32, xv.

19. Père Chauchetière quoted in Hugh Honour, "The Noble Savage," in *The European Vision of America* (Cleveland: Cleveland Museum of Art, 1975), 195.

20. Brian Dippie, *The Vanishing American: White Attitudes and U.S. Indian Policy* (Middletown, CT: Wesleyan University Press, 1982), 20.

21. Owen to Leland, 20 September 1898 and 5 November 1898. (HSP).

22. W[illaim]. W[ells]. N[ewell]., review of *The Daughter of Alouette, Journal of American, Folklore* 10, no. 38 (July–September, 1897): 250–51.

23. Owen to Leland, 27 November 1895 (HSP); Leland to Owen, 16 June 1893, Pannell, *Charles Godfrey Leland*, 366–67.

24. Owen to Leland, 5 November 1898 (HSP).

25. Owen to Leland, 5 November 1898 (HSP).

26. Owen to Leland, 8 March 1899 (HSP).

27. Owen to Leland, 20 September 1898 (HSP).

28. Mueller, *Daring to Be Different*, 80–92.

29. Owen to Leland, 22 May 1898 (HSP).

30. Owen to Leland, 16 August 1898 and 30 November 1899 (HSP).

31. Owen to Leland, 26 June 1902 (HSP).

Chapter 7

1. "Treaty with the Sauk and Foxes, 1804," in Kappler, ed., *Indian Affairs,* vol. 2, 74–77.

2. Robert E. Parkin, *Tales of Black Hawk* (St. Louis: St. Louis Genealogical Society, 1974), 139.

3. Milo Milton Quaife, ed., *Life of Black Hawk* (New York: Dover, 1994), 65–69.

4. Quaife, ed. *Life of Black Hawk,* 70–75.

5. Johnathan L. Buffalo, "A Collection of Observations Relating to the Meskwaki Tribe," in Mary Bennett, Johnathan Lanz Buffalo, and Dawn Suzanne Wanatee, eds., *Meskwaki History,* CD-ROM (Iowa City: State Historical Society of Iowa, 2004).

6. Kappler, ed., "Treaty with the Iowa, Etc. 1836," and "Treaty with the Oto, Etc. 1836," *Indian Affairs,* vol. 2: 468–70, 479–81.

7. Owen, *Old Rabbit,* 169–79.

8. Owen, "Among the Voodoos," 246.

9. Owen, "Among the Voodoos," 248.

10. Rosaldo, *Culture and Truth,* 30–31.

11. Schmitz, *White Robe's Dilemma,* 61–68. Sandra Kay Massey, email correspondence with the author, 11 February 2007; Eberle, *The Incredible Owen Girls,* 32.

12. Mable D. Thompson, "Indian Collection at the State Museum," *Missouri Magazine* 4 (November 1930): 12; Mary Lasley, "Sac and Fox Tales," *Journal of American Folk Lore* 15, no. 58 (July–September 1902): 170–78.

13. Owen, *Folk-lore of the Musquakie,* 30–31.

14. Owen, *Folk-lore of the Musquakie,* 56.

15. Owen, *Folk-lore of the Musquakie,* 40, 54.

16. Schmitz, *White Robe's Dilemma,* 68.

17. Email correspondence, Sandra Kaye Massey to the author, 11 February 2007.

18. Correspondence, Jimm GoodTracks to Elaine Schroeter, 3 September 1995, electronic copy, collection of the author; Owen, *Folk-lore of the Musquakie,* 135–39.

19. "Anthropologic Miscellanea: Muskwaki Indians of Iowa," *American Anthropologist* 7 (1905): 575.

20. Owen, *Folk-lore of the Musquakie,* 22–23.

21. Edward L. Purcell, "The Mesquakie Indian Settlement in 1905," *Iowa Heritage Illustrated* 85 (2004): 92–103; "The Ward-Mesquakie Photograph Collection," *Iowa Heritage Illustrated* 85 (2004): 104–15; Duren Ward, "Meskwakia," *Iowa Journal of History and Politics* 4 (1906): 179–89.

22. Dan L. Trapp, "William Jones," *Encyclopedia of Frontier Biography* (Lincoln: University of Nebraska Press, 1991), 744; William Jones, "Fox Texts," *Publications of the American Ethnological Society* 1 (1907); "Native, Anthropologist, and Native Anthropologist: William Jones and the Making of *Fox Texts*," Meskwaki Education NetWork Initiative (http://www.menwi.org/index.html, accessed 4 February 2008).

23. Johnathan Lanz Buffalo quoted in Sophilia Keahna, "William Jones," in Bennett, Buffalo, and Wanatee, eds., *Meskwaki History*.

24. Owen to Burrill, May 1931, WHMC-C; Owen, *Folk-Lore of the Musquakie*, 40, 54, 56.

25. Correspondence, Owen to Leland, 27 September 1902 and 29 September 1899 (HSP).

26. Correspondence, Leland to Owen, 13 August 1902, in Pannell, *Charles Godfrey Leland*, 420.

27. Owen to Leland, 27 September 1902 (HSP); Aleš Hrdlička, "The Lansing Skeleton," *American Anthropologist* 5, no. 2 (April–June, 1903): 323–30.

28. Klaus Lubbers, *Born for the Shade: Stereotypes of the Native American in United States Literature and the Visual Arts, 1776–1894* (Amsterdam: Rodopi, 1994), 32; Roy Harvey Pearce, *Savagism and Civilization: A Study of the Indian and the American Mind* (Baltimore: John Hopkins University Press, 1967), 4.

29. John Benjamin Sanborn quoted in Thomas King, *The Truth about Stories: A Native Narrative* (Minneapolis: University of Minnesota Press, 2005), 83–84.

30. Heartland, preface to *Folk-lore of the Musquakie*, vi.

31. Owen, *Folk-lore of the Musquakie*, 31–32.

32. Owen, *Folk-lore of the Musquakie*, 95, 138, 140, 143.

33. Owen, *Folk-lore of the Musquakie*, 34, 114, 121, 138, 142.

34. Owen, *Folk-lore of the Musquakie*, 29.

35. Owen, *Folk-lore of the Musquakie*, 78.

36. Owen, *Folk-lore of the Musquakie*, 77–86.

37. A. Hingston, "Review of *Folklore of the Musquakie Indians*," *Man* 6 (1906): 29.

Chapter 8

1. Owen to Leland, 30 July 1902 (HSP).

2. *Ibid.*

3. Leland to Owen, October 1902 and 13 August 1902, in Pannell, *Charles Godfrey Leland*, 420, 421.

4. Owen to Mrs. John Harrison, 22 March 1903 (HSP); Pannell, *Charles Godfrey Leland*, 424–25.

5. Owen to Leland, 8 June 1900 (HSP).

6. Owen to Leland, 29 September 1899 (HSP).

7. Owen to Leland, 29 September 1899 (HSP).

8. *Year Book, 1915–1916* (St. Joseph, MO: City Federation of Women's Clubs, 1916).

9. Susan L. Pentlin and Rebecca B. Schroeder, "H. M. Belden: The English Club, and the Missouri Folk-Lore Society," *Missouri Folklore Society Journal* 8–9 (1986–1987): 1–8.

10. The Constitution of the Missouri Folk-Lore Society as quoted in Pentlin and Schroeder, "H. M. Belden: The English Club, and the Missouri Folk-Lore Society," 6.

11. Mary Alicia Owen, "Suggestions for Collectors of Negro and Indian Folk-Lore in Missouri," undated publication of the Missouri Folklore Soci-

ety, Missouri Folklore Society Collection (2045), State Historical Society of Missouri.

12. Eberle, *The Incredible Owen Girls*, 66.

13. Mary Alicia Owen, *The Sacred Council Hills* (St. Joseph, MO: self-published, 1909), 6.

14. Owen, *The Sacred Council Hills*, 18.

15. Owen, *The Sacred Council Hills*, 26, 29.

16. Owen, *The Sacred Council Hills*, 34.

17. "Mrs. Owen Dead," *St. Joseph Gazette*, 16 December 1911, 10.

18. Owen to Leland, 20 September 1898 (HSP).

19. "Today's American Woman: She Knows All about Indian Folklore and Magic," *Tacoma (Washington) Times*, 16 February 1911.

20. Benjamin W. Bacon, "The Leiden Congress for the History of Religion," *American Journal of Theology* 17, no. 1 (January 1913): 80–89: Eberle, *The Incredible Owen Girls*, 141–44.

21. Pentlin and Schroeder, "H. M. Belden: The English Club, and the Missouri Folk-Lore Society," 8, 10.

22. Mary Alicia Owen, "Legends of St. Joseph," *St. Joseph Gazette*, 3 December 1916, 18.

23. Jessie Hawkins Cockburn, "Twelfth Installment of The House of Thirteen Windows: Written by the Mary Alicia Owen Story Tellers League," *St. Joseph Observer*, 13 April 1918.

24. Mary Alicia Owen, "St. Joseph's Sweet Singer," *St. Joseph Observer*, 13 November 1918.

25. Bronner, *Folklife Studies from the Gilded Age*, 39–40.

26. Pentlin and Schroeder, "H. M. Belden: The English Club, and the Missouri Folk-Lore Society," 14, 16.

27. Mary Alicia Owen, "Social Customs and Usages in Missouri during the Last Century," *Missouri Historical Review* 15 (October 1920): 176–90.

28. Mary Alicia Owen, "The Road to Paradise," 3–7.

29. Poll book, 1 Ward, 1 Precinct, City of Hannibal, Mason Township, Marion County, Missouri, Tuesday 31 August 1920, manuscript collection number 5, Missouri State Archives; notice of the Democratic Women's Club meeting, *St. Joseph Observer*, 2 October 1920; "Democratic Meetings Next Week," *St. Joseph Observer*, 17 October 1922.

30. "Legends of the Hill," *St. Joseph News-Press*, 13 March 1926, 3.

31. Robert M. Snyder Jr., "A Lost Legend of Missouri," *Kansas City Times*, 19 January 1935.

32. Mary Alicia Owen, "Love Story of Faraon, Most Carefree of the Robidioux Boys," undated newspaper clipping, Archive of Women Writers, Missouri Western State University.

33. Author unknown, "St. Joseph Indians," typewritten manuscript, Mary Alicia Owen vertical file, St. Joseph Public Library. While the author of this manuscript is not known, the writer discusses working on an article about Lanowah Park in St. Joseph. In 1923, Charles K. Soper published an article about the park that was clearly influenced by Owen. See Charles K. Soper, "Wawalanowa: Land of the Road to Paradise," *Missouri Historical Review* 20, no. 2 (January 1926): 217–22.

34. "Report of the Resources Museum Commission," *Official Manual, State of Missouri, 1931–1932* (Jefferson City, MO: State of Missouri, 1931), 676; Thompson, "Indian Collection in the State Museum," 9, 12.

35. "Luella Owen Dead," *St. Joseph News-Press*, 1 June 1932.

36. Map 44 (1911), map 43 (1897), map 17 (1888), map 8, 1883, "St. Joseph, Missouri," 1883–1911, Sanborn Fire Insurance Maps.

37. "Mary Alicia Owen, Noted Folklorist, Died This Morning," *St. Joseph News-Press*, 5 January 1935, 1.

38. Ibid.; "Friends Pay Last Tribute to Miss Owen," *St. Joseph Gazette*, 6 January 1935, 2A.

39. Mary Alicia Owen, certificate of death, Buchanan County, Missouri, 20 February 1935, certificate #204, Missouri State Archives.

40. "Friends Pay Last Tribute to Miss Owen," *St. Joseph Gazette*, 6 January 1935, 2A; "Mary Alicia Owen, Noted Folklorist, Died This Morning," *St. Joseph News-Press*, 5 January 1935, 1.

Epilogue

1. W. K. McNeil, *The Charm Is Broken: Readings in Arkansas and Missouri Folklore* (Little Rock: August House, 1984), 139.

2. Alan R. Havig, ed., *Filling Leisure Hours: Essays from the Missouri Historical Review* (Columbia: State Historical Society of Missouri, 2006).

3. Mary Alicia Owen, "The Road to Paradise," City of St. Joseph, Missouri, c. 2010, Courtesy of the St. Joseph Parks, Recreation, and Civic Facilities Department; "Sacred Land" PowerPoint presentation, St. Joseph Parks, Recreation, and Civic Facilities Department.

4. Owen, "The Road to Paradise," *The Midwest Bookman*, 4.

5. Michael J. O'Brien, *Paradigms of the Past: The Story of Missouri Archaeology* (Columbia: University of Missouri Press, 1996), 22; Michael J. O'Brien and W. Raymond Wood, *The Prehistory of Missouri* (Columbia: University of Missouri Press, 1998), 144.

6. Alanson Skinner, "Ethnology of the Ioway and Sauk Indians," *Bulletin of the Public Museum of the City of Milwaukee* 5 (1923–1926): 37, 255.

7. Skinner, "Ethnology of the Ioway and Sauk Indians," 256.

8. Charles K. Soper, "Wawalanowa, Land of the Road to Paradise," *Missouri Historical Review* 20, no. 2 (January 1926): 221.

9. John Pickard, *Report of the Capitol Decoration Commission, 1917–1928* (Jefferson City, MO: Hugh Stephens Press, 1928), 108–11.

10. Logan, Sheridan A. *Old St. Jo: Gateway to the West, 1799–1932* (St. Joseph, MO[?]: John Sublett Logan Foundation, 1979), 16.

11. Claudia J. H. Packer, "The Story of the Chief White Cloud Sculpture," courtesy of the St. Joseph Parks, Recreation, and Civic Facilities Department; souvenir program, Platte Purchase Commemoration, 5 July 2004, courtesy of the St. Joseph Parks, Recreation, and Civic Facilities Department.

12. Henry Wadsworth Longfellow, "Hiawatha: A Poem," 1856.

13. Jean M. O'Brien, *Firsting and Lasting: Writing Indians Out of Existence in New England* (Minneapolis: University of Minnesota Press, 2010), 6–7, 55–56.

Bibliography

Works by Mary Alicia Owen

Owen, Mary Alicia. "Among the Voodoos." In Joseph Jacobs and Alfred Nutt, eds., *The International Folk Lore Congress, 1891: Papers and Transactions*. London: David Nutt, 1892: 230–48.

———. "The Bride's Farewell." *Prairie Farmer* 41 (26 February 1870): 62

———. "Coyote and Little Pig." *Journal of American Folklore* 15, no. 56 (January–March 1902): 63–65.

———. *The Daughter of Alouette*. London: Methuen and Company, 1896.

———. *Folk-lore of the Musquakie Indians of North America and Catalogue of Musquakie Beadwork and Other Objects in the Collection of the Folk-Lore Society*. London: D. Nutt, 1904.

———. "The Folklorist." Typed manuscript. Vertical file: Biography: Owen, Mary Alicia. St. Joseph Public Library.

———. "The Homesick Missourian." *St. Joseph Observer*. 1 April 1916. 1.

———. "Legends of Prospect Hill." *St. Joseph News-Press*. 13 March 1926. 3.

———. "Legends of St. Joseph." 3 December 1916. Newspaper clipping. Vertical file: Biography: Owen, Mary Alicia. St. Joseph Public Library.

———. "Love Story of Faraon: Most Carefree of the Robidoux Boys." Undated newspaper clipping. Archive of Women Writers. Missouri Western State University Library.

———. *Old Rabbit, the Voodoo, and Other Sorcerers*. 1893. Reprint, North Stratford, NH: Ayer Company Publishers, 1999.

———. "Ole Rabbit an' de dawg he stole." *Journal of American Folk-Lore* 3 (April 1890): 135–38.

———. "Pig-tail Charley: Negro Tale." *Journal of American Folk-Lore* 16 (January 1903), 58–60.

———. "Poor Lucy." Archive of Women Writers along the Rivers Project, Special Collection, Missouri Western State University Library, St. Joseph, Missouri.

———. "The Road to Paradise." Midwest Bookman 3 (1921): 3–7.

———. *The Sacred Council Hills: A Folk-Lore Drama*. St. Joseph, MO: self-published, 1909.

———. "The Significance of Folk-Lore (abstract). *Missouri State Teachers' Association Bulletin* 2, no. 1 (January 1916): 85–86.

———. "Three Little Pigs: Story." *Journal of American Folk-Lore* 15 (January 1902): 64–65.

———. "Three Stories." *The Folklorist* 1 (July 1893): 101–6.

———. "St. Joseph's Sweet Singer." *St. Joseph Observer* (30 November 1918).

———. "Social Customs and Usages in Missouri During the Last Century." *Missouri Historical Review* (October 1920).

———. "Suggestions for Collector of Negro and Indian Lore." Undated publication of the Missouri Folklore Society. Missouri Folklore Society Collection (2045). State Historical Society of Missouri–Columbia.

———. "The Taming of Tarias." *The Century* 39 (December 1889).

———. "Voodooism." In Helen Wheeler Bassett, and Frederick Star, eds. *The International Folk-Lore Congress of the World's Columbian Exposition*. Chicago: Charles H. Sergel, 1898.

Scott, Julia (Mary Alicia Owen). "The Exile's Daughter." *Godey's Lady's Book and Magazine* 111, no. 663 (September 1885); and *The Massachusetts Ploughman and New England Journal of Agriculture* 44, no. 48 (29 June 1885): 4.

———. "Jack in Search of Jill." *Peterson's Magazine* 86, no. 3 (September 1884): 243.

———. "Miss Dolly's Ideals." *Ballou's Monthly Magazine* 65, no. 6 (June 1887): 499.

———. "The New Tenor." *Frank Leslie's Popular Monthly* 29, no. 5 (May 1890): 609.

———. "Patty's Literary Experiences." *Ballou's Monthly Magazine* 60 (July 1884): 83.

———. "Phoebus or Cupid?" *Overland Magazine* 8, no. 44 (August 1886): 129.

Unconfirmed works by Mary Alicia Owen (mentioned in various sources, but not located)

Owen, Mary Alicia. "Captain Charles' Burgoo Party."

———. "Home Life of Squaws."

———. "Jim's Salvationer."

———. "Messiah Beliefs of the American Indians."

———. "Old Settlers of St. Joseph."

———. "Oracles and Witches." 1902.

———. *An Ozark Gypsy*. Possibly published in London by T. Fisher Unwin. c. 1899.

———. "Pioneers of the Platte Purchase."

———. "Rain Gods of the American Indians." 1912.

———. "Rhymes of Various Things."

Archival Collections

Archive of Women Writers along the Rivers Project, Special Collection, Missouri Western State University Library, St. Joseph, Missouri.

Great Nemaha Agency Files. National Archives Microfilm Publication M234, Roll 307.

Letters received by the Office of Indian Affairs, 1824–1881. Record Group 75.

Owen, Mary Alicia (to Charles Leland), Historical Society of Pennsylvania Society small collection (Collection 22B), Historical Society of Pennsylvania.

Rebecca and Adolph Schroeder Papers. Collection WUNP 5643. State Historical Society–Columbia.

Robert McClure Snyder Jr. Papers, 1890–1937. Collection C3524. State Historical Society of Missouri–Columbia.

Manuscript Collection. Missouri State Archives.

Missouri Death Certificate Database. Missouri State Archives. http://www.sos.mo.gov/archives/resources/deathcertificates/.

"Missouri Slave Schedules." *Population Schedules of the Seventh Census of the United States.* National Archives Microfilm Publication M432, roll 422. United States Bureau of the Census.

"Missouri Slave Schedules." *Population Schedules of the Eighth Census of the United States,* vol. 1. National Archives Microfilm Publication M653, roll 661. United States Bureau of the Census.

Missouri State Archives Soldiers' Records Database. http://www.sos.mo.gov/archives/soldiers/.

Missouri Supreme Court files. Missouri State Archives.

Owen, Mary Alicia. Notes for a catalogue of Owen's collection of Mesquakie artifacts. Photocopy of original handwritten document, Missouri State Museum, Jefferson City, Missouri.

St. Louis Circuit Court files. Missouri State Archives–St. Louis.

Union Provost Marshals' File of Papers Relating to Individual Citizens, 1861–1866. National Archives Microfilm M345, roll F1607. War Department Collection of Confederate Records. Record Group 109.

"The Sanborn Fire Insurance Map Collection." University of Missouri Digital Library. http//digital.library.umsystem.edu/.

"1850 Missouri Census for Buchanan, Butler, Caldwell, and Callaway counties." *Population Schedules of the Seventh Census of the United States.* National Archives Microfilm Publication M432, roll 393. United States Bureau of the Census.

Newspapers

Hocking Sentinel (Logan, Ohio)
Hopkinsville Kentuckian
Kansas City Star
St. Joseph (Missouri) Gazette
St. Joseph (Missouri) News-Press
St. Joseph (Missouri) Observer
New York Times
Tacoma (Washington) Times
Times (London)

Books and Articles

Abel, Annie Heloise. *The American Indian as Slaveholder and Secessionist.* Lincoln: University of Nebraska Press, 1992.

Allcorn, Mary Elizabeth. "Mary Alicia Owen: Missouri Folklorist." *Missouri Folklore Society Journal* 8–9 (1986–1987): 71–78.

Anderson, Jeffrey E. *Conjure in American Society.* Baton Rouge: Louisiana State University Press, 2005.

"Anthropologic Miscellanea: Muskwaki Indians of Iowa." *American Anthropologist* 7 (1905).

Bacon, Benjamin W. "The Leiden Congress for the History of Religion." *American Journal of Theology* 17. No. 1 (January 1913): 80–89.

Barnett, Louise. The Ignoble Savage: American Literary Racism, 1790–1890. Westport, CT: Greenwood, 1975.

Barry, Louise. *The Beginning of the West: Annals of the Kansas Gateway to the American West, 1540–1854.* Topeka: Kansas State Historical Society, 1972.

Bassett, Fletcher S. "Notes on Folklore Collecting," (1890, 1893). In Simon J. Bronner. *Folklife Studies From the Gilded Age: Object, Rite, and Custom in Victorian America,* Ann Arbor, MI: UMI Research Press, 1987.

Bassett, Helen Wheeler, and Frederick Starr, eds. *The International Folk-Lore Congress of the World's Columbian Exposition.* Chicago: Charles H. Sergel, 1898.

Bataille, Gretchen M., David Mayer Grandwohl, and Charles L. P. Silet, eds. *The Worlds Between Two Rivers: Perspectives on American Indians in Iowa.* Iowa City: University of Iowa Press, 2000.

Bennett, Mary, Johnathan Lanz Buffalo, and Dawn Suzanne Wanatee. *Meskwaki History.* CD-ROM. Iowa City: State Historical Society of Iowa, 2004.

Berkhofer, Robert F., Jr. *The White Man's Indian: Images of the American Indian from Columbus to the Present.* New York: Knopf, 1978.

Berry, Jason. *The Spirit of Black Hawk: A Mystery of Africans and Indians,* Jackson: University Press of Mississippi, 1995.

Bird, S. Elizabeth, ed. *Dressing in Feathers: The Construction of the Indian in American Popular Culture.* Boulder, CO: Westview, 1996.

Blaine, Martha Royce. *The Ioway Indians.* Norman: University of Oklahoma Press, 1995.

Brandone-Falcone, Janice. "Constance Runcie and the Runcie Club of St. Joseph." In Thomas M. Spencer, ed., *The Other Missouri*

History: Populists, Prostitutes and Regular Folks. Columbia: University of Missouri Press, 2004.

Bronner, Simon J. *American Folklore Studies: An Intellectual History*. Lawrence: University Press of Kansas, 1986.

———, ed. *Consuming Visions: Accumulation and Display of Goods in America 1880–1920*. New York: W. W. Norton, 1989.

———. "The Early Movements of Anthropology and Their Folkloristic Relationships." *Folklore* 95 (1984) 57–73.

———, ed. *Folklife Studies From the Gilded Age: Object, Rite, and Custom in Victorian America*, Ann Arbor, MI: UMI Research Press, 1987.

Brown, Alison K. "Beads, Belts, and Bands: The Mesquakie Collection of Mary Alicia Owen." *Missouri Folklore Society Journal* 18–19 (1996–1997): 25–44.

———. "Collecting Material Folklore: Motivations and Methods in the Owen and Hasluck Collections." *Folklore* 109 (1998): 33–40.

Buchanan County and St. Joseph. St. Joseph, MO: St. Joseph Publishing, c. 1900.

Carneiro, Robert L. *Evolutionism in Cultural Anthropology*. Boulder, CO: Westview, 2003.

Cary, Elizabeth Luther. "Recent Writings by American Indians." *The Book Buyer*. 1902, Internet, University of Virginia Library, http://etext.lib.virginia.edu/toc/modeng/public/Car-Rece.html: 21–25.

Carr, Helen. *Inventing the American Primitive: Politics, Gender and the Representation of Native American Literary Traditions, 1789–1936*. New York: New York University Press, 1996.

Clements, William M. *Native American Verbal Art: Texts and Contexts*. Tucson: University of Arizona Press, 1996.

Coy, Roy E. and Mrs. Walter Hall. "The Genealogy of the White Cloud Family." *Museum Graphic* 9 (Spring 1952).

The Daily News' History of Buchanan County. St. Joseph, MO: St. Joseph Publishing, 1898.

Daniels, Elizabeth. *History of Vassar College*. Internet: http://historian.vassar.edu/chronology/1861–1870.

Darnell, Regna. *Invisible Genealogies: A History of Americanist Anthropology*. Lincoln: University of Nebraska Press, 2001.

Dippie, Brian. *The Vanishing American: White Attitudes and U.S. Indian Policy.* Middletown, CT: Wesleyan University Press, 1982.

D[orsey], J[ames]. O[wen]. Review of *Old Rabbit, the Voodoo, and Other Sorcerers*, by Mary Alicia Owen. *Journal of American Folklore* 6 (October–December 1893): 322–24.

Dorson, Richard M. "American Folklorists in Britain." *Journal of the Folklore Institute* 7, no. 2/3 (August–December 1970).

Eberle, Jean Fahey. *The Incredible Owen Girls.* St. Louis: Boar's Head Press, 1977.

Ellingson, Ter. *The Myth of the Noble Savage.* Berkley: University of California Press, 2001.

Etcheson, Nicole. *Bleeding Kansas: Contested Liberty in the Civil War Era.* Lawrence: University Press of Kansas, 2004.

Filbert, Preston. *The Half Not Told: The Civil War in a Frontier Town.* Mechanicsburg, PA: Stackpole Books, 2001.

Garrett, Aaron. "Anthropology: The Origin of Human Nature." In Alexander Brodie, ed. *The Cambridge Companion to the Scottish Enlightenment.* New York: Cambridge University Press, 2003.

Gussow, Zachary. *Sac and Fox and Iowa Indians.* Vol. 1. New York: Garland, 1974.

Halliburton, Rudi. *Red Over Black: Black Slavery Among the Cherokee Indians.* Westport: Greenwood, 1977.

Hearne, Joanna. "The Cross-Heart People: Race and Inheritance in the Silent Western." *Journal of Popular film and Television* 30, no. 4 (Winter 2003).

Heartland, E. Sydney. Review of *Old Rabbit, the Voodoo, and Other Sorcerers*, by Mary Alicia Owen. *Folklore* 5 (March 1894): 72–73.

Hinsley, Curtis M., Jr. *Savages and Scientists: The Smithsonian Institution and the Development of American Anthropology, 1846–1910.* Washington, DC: Smithsonian Institution Press, 1981.

Hewitt, J. N. B. ed. *Journal of Rudolph Friederich Kurz.* Lincoln: University of Nebraska Press, 1970.

Hingston, A. "Review of *Folklore of the Musquakie Indians.*" *Man* 6 (1906): 29.

The History of Buchanan County Missouri. St. Joseph: Union Historical Company, 1881.

"The International Folklore Congress, 1891." *Folk-Lore* 2. No. 3 (September 1891).

Honour, Hugh. "The Noble Savage." In *The European Vision of America*. Cleveland: Cleveland Museum of Art, 1975.

Hrdlička, Aleš. "The Lansing Skeleton." *American Anthropologist* 5, no. 2 (April–June, 1903): 323–30.

Jahoda, Gustav. *Images of Savage: Ancient Roots of Modern Prejudice in Western Culture*. London: Routledge, 1999.

James, George Warton. *What The White Race May Learn From The Indian*. Chicago: Forbes and Company, 1908.

Johnson, Joan Marie. *Southern Women at Vassar: The Poppenheim Family Letters, 1882–1916*. Columbia: University of South Carolina Press, 2002.

Johnson, Willard R. "Tracing Trails of Blood on Ice: Commemorating 'The Great Escape' in 1861–62 of Indians and Blacks into Kansas." *Negro History Bulletin* 64 (2001).

Jones, William. *Fox Texts*. Leyden: E. J. Brill, 1907.

Kaplan, Amy and Donald E. Pease, eds. *Cultures of U.S. Imperialism*. Durham, NC: Duke University Press, 1993.

Kappler, Charles J., ed. *Indian Affairs: Laws and Treaties*. Vol. 2. Washington, DC: Government Printing Office, 1904.

Karttunen, Francis. *Between Worlds: Interpreters, Guides, and Survivors*. New Brunswick, NJ: Rutgers University Press, 1994.

Katz, William Loren. *Black Indians: A Hidden Heritage*. New York: Athenaeum, 1986.

King, Thomas. *The Truth About Stories: A Native Narrative*. Minneapolis: University of Minnesota Press, 2005.

Kuklick, Henrika. *The Savage Within: The Social History of British Anthropology, 1885–1945*. Cambridge: Cambridge University Press, 1991.

Lavender, Catherine J. *Scientists and Storytellers: Feminist Anthropologists and the Construction of the American Southwest*. Albuquerque: University of New Mexico Press, 2006.

Lasley, Mary. "Sac and Fox Tales." *Journal of American Folk Lore* 15, no. 58 (July–September 1902).

Leland, Charles Godfrey. *The Algonquin Legends of New England, Or, Myths and Folk Lore of the Micmac, Passamaquoddy, and Penobscot Tribes*. Boston: Houghton, Mifflin and Company, 1884.

———. *Memoirs*. Vol. 1. London: William Heinemann, 1894.

Letters from Old Time Vassar: Written by a Student in 1869–1870. Poughkeepsie, NY: Vassar College, 1915.

Linner, Edward R. *Vassar: The Remarkable Growth of a Man and His College, 1855–1865.* Poughkeepsie, NY: Vassar College, 1984.

Logan, Sheridan A. *Old St. Jo: Gateway to the West, 1799–1932.* St. Joseph, MO [?]: John Sublett Logan Foundation, 1979.

Lubbers, Klaus. *Born for the Shade: Stereotypes of the Native American in United States Literature and the Visual Arts, 1776–1894.* Amsterdam: Rodopi, 1994.

March, David D. "Charles D. Drake and the Constitutional Convention of 1865." *The Civil War in Missouri: Essays From the Missouri Historical Review, 1906–2006.* Columbia: State Historical Society of Missouri, 2006.

McKenney, Thomas L. and James Hall. "Young Mahaska." *History of the Indian Tribes of North America.* Vol. 2. Philadelphia: D. Rice and A. N. Hart, 1855.

McNeil, William K. "Mary Alicia Owen, Collection of Afro-American and Indian Lore in Missouri." *Missouri Folklore Society Journal* 2 (1980): 1–14.

The Meskwaki Education NetWork Initiative. Internet, http://www.menwi.org/index.html.

Mueller, Doris Land. *Daring to Be Different: Missouri's Remarkable Owen Sisters.* Columbia: University of Missouri Press, 2010.

Murray, David. *Matter, Magic, and Spirit: Representing Indian and African American Belief.* Philadelphia: University of Pennsylvania Press, 2007.

Nash, Roderick. *Wilderness and the American Mind.* New Haven: Yale University Press, 1967.

Neely, Jeremy. *The Border Between Them: Violence and Reconciliation on the Kansas-Missouri Line.* Columbia: University of Missouri Press, 2007.

N[ewell]., W[illaim]. W[ells]. Review of *The Daughter of Alouette. The Journal of American, Folklore* 10, No. 38 (July–September, 1897). 250–51.

Olson, Greg. *The Ioway in Missouri.* Columbia: University of Missouri Press, 2008.

———. "Two Portraits, Two Legacies: Anglo American Artists View Chief White Cloud." *Gateway* 25 (summer 2004): 20–31.

Oring, Elliot, *Folk Groups and Folklore Genres: An Introduction.* Logan: Utah State University Press, 1986.

Parkhill, Thomas. *Weaving Ourselves into the Land: Charles Godfrey Leland, "Indians" and the Study of Native American Religions.* Albany: State University of New York Press, 1997.

Parkin, Robert E. *Tales of Black Hawk.* St. Louis: St. Louis Genealogical Society, 1974.

Parry, Ellwood. *The Image of the Indian and the Black Man in American Art, 1590–1900.* New York: George Brazillier, 1974.

Pearce, Roy Harvey. *Savagism and Civilization: A Study of the Indian and the American Mind.* Baltimore: John Hopkins University Press, 1967.

Pennell, Elizabeth Robins. *Charles Godfrey Leland: A Biography.* 1906. Reprint, Freeport, NY: Books for Libraries Press, 1970.

Pentlin, Susan L. and Rebecca B. Schroeder. "H. M. Belden: The English Club, and the Missouri Folk-Lore Society." *Missouri Folklore Society Journal* VIII–IX (1986–1987). 1–8.

Peyer, Bernd C., ed. *The Singing Spirit: Early Short Stories by North American Indians.* Tucson: University of Arizona Press, 1989.

Prucha, Francis Paul. *The Indians in American Society: From the Revolutionary War to the Present.* Berkeley: University of California Press, 1985.

Purcell, L. Edward. "The Mesquakie Indian Settlement in 1905." *Iowa Heritage Illustrated* 85 (2004).

———. "The Ward-Mesquakie Photograph Collection." *Iowa Heritage Illustrated* 85 (2004).

Quiafe, Milo Milton, ed. *Life of Black Hawk.* New York: Dover, 1994.

"Resources Museum Commission." *Official Manual of the State of Missouri 1931–1932*: 676.

"Richard Anthony Proctor." *Monthly Notices of the Royal Astronomical Society* 49 (February 1889).

Rogers, Sherbrooke. *Sarah Josepha Hale: A New England Pioneer, 1788–1879.* Grantham, NH: Tompson and Rutter, 1985.

Rosaldo, Renato. *Culture and Truth: The Remaking of Social Analysis.* Boston: Beacon Press, 1993.

Sanderson, Stephen K. *Social Evolutionism: A Critical History.* Cambridge, MA: Blackwell, 1990.

Schmitz, Neil. *White Robe's Dilemma: Tribal History in American Literature.* Amherst: University of Massachusetts, 2001.

Shoemaker, Floyd Calvin, ed. *Missouri and Missourians: Land of Contrast and People of Achievements.* Vol. 4. Chicago: Lewis Publishing: 1943.

Smith, Henry Nash. "The Scribbling Women and the Cosmic Success Story." *Critical Inquiry* 1, no. 1 (September 1974).

Soper, Charles K. "Wawalanowa, Land of the Road to Paradise." *Missouri Historical Review* 20 (January 1926): 217–22.

Stocking, George W. *After Tylor: British Social Anthropology, 1888–1951.* Madison: University of Wisconsin Press, 1995.

———. *Victorian Anthropology.* New York: Free Press, 1987.

Thompson, Mable D. "Indian Collection in the State Museum." *Missouri Magazine* 4 (November 1930): 9–13.

Thorne, Tanis C. *The Many Hands of My Relations: French and Indians on the Lower Missouri.* Columbia: University of Missouri Press, 1996.

Thwaites, Reuben Gold. *Early Western Travels, 1748–1846.* Cleveland: Arthur H. Clark, 1906.

Togovnick, Marianna. *Gone Primitive, Savage Intellects, Modern Lives.* Chicago: University of Chicago Press, 1991.

Trachtenberg, Alan. *Shades of Hiawatha: Staging Indian, Making Americans.* New York: Hill and Wang, 2004.

———. *The Incorporation of America: Culture and Society in the Gilded Age.* New York: Hill and Wang, 1982.

Tracy, W. P. *Men Who Make St. Joseph "The City Worth While."* Self published, n.d. (c. 1920).

Trapp, Dan L. "William Jones." *Encyclopedia of Frontier Biography.* Lincoln: University of Nebraska Press, 1991.

Turner, Frederick Jackson. "The Significance of the Frontier in American History." In *The Frontier in American History.* New York: Dover, 1996.

Vest, Jay Hansford C. "From Bobtail to Brer Rabbit: Native American influences on Uncle Remus." *American Indian Quarterly* 24, no. 1 (winter 2000): 19–43.

Ward, Duren. "Historico-anthropological Possibilities in Iowa." *Iowa Journal of History and Politics* 1 (1903).

———. "Meskwakia." *Iowa Journal of History and Politics* 4 (1906).

———. "The Meskwaki People of Today." *Iowa Journal of History and Politics* 4 (1906).

Whites, LeeAnn. *Gender Matters: Civil War, Reconstruction, and the Making of the New South*. New York: Palgrave MacMillan, 2005.

Wiebe, Robert H. *The Search for Order, 1877–1920*. New York: Hill and Wang, 1995.

Williams, Walter. *History of Northwest Missouri*. Vol. 2. Chicago: Lewis Publishing, 1915.

Willoughby, Robert J. Robidoux's Town: A Nineteenth-Century History of St. Joseph, Missouri, Westphalia, MO: Westphalia Printing, 1997.

Year Book, 1915–1916. St. Joseph: City Federation of Women's Clubs, 1916.

Yronwode, Catherine. ed. *Ghostly Voices from Dixieland*. Internet, http://www.southern-spirits.com.

Zumwalt, Rosemary Levy. *American Folklore Scholarship: A Dialogue of Dissent*. Bloomington: Indian University Press, 1988.

Index